AUG

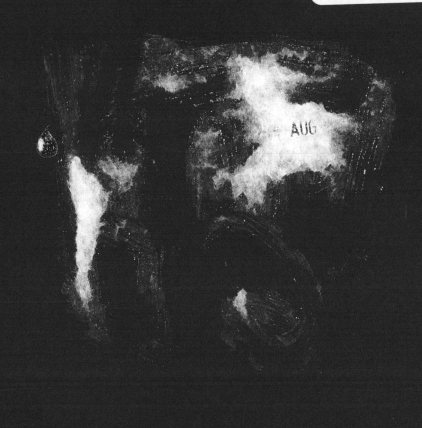

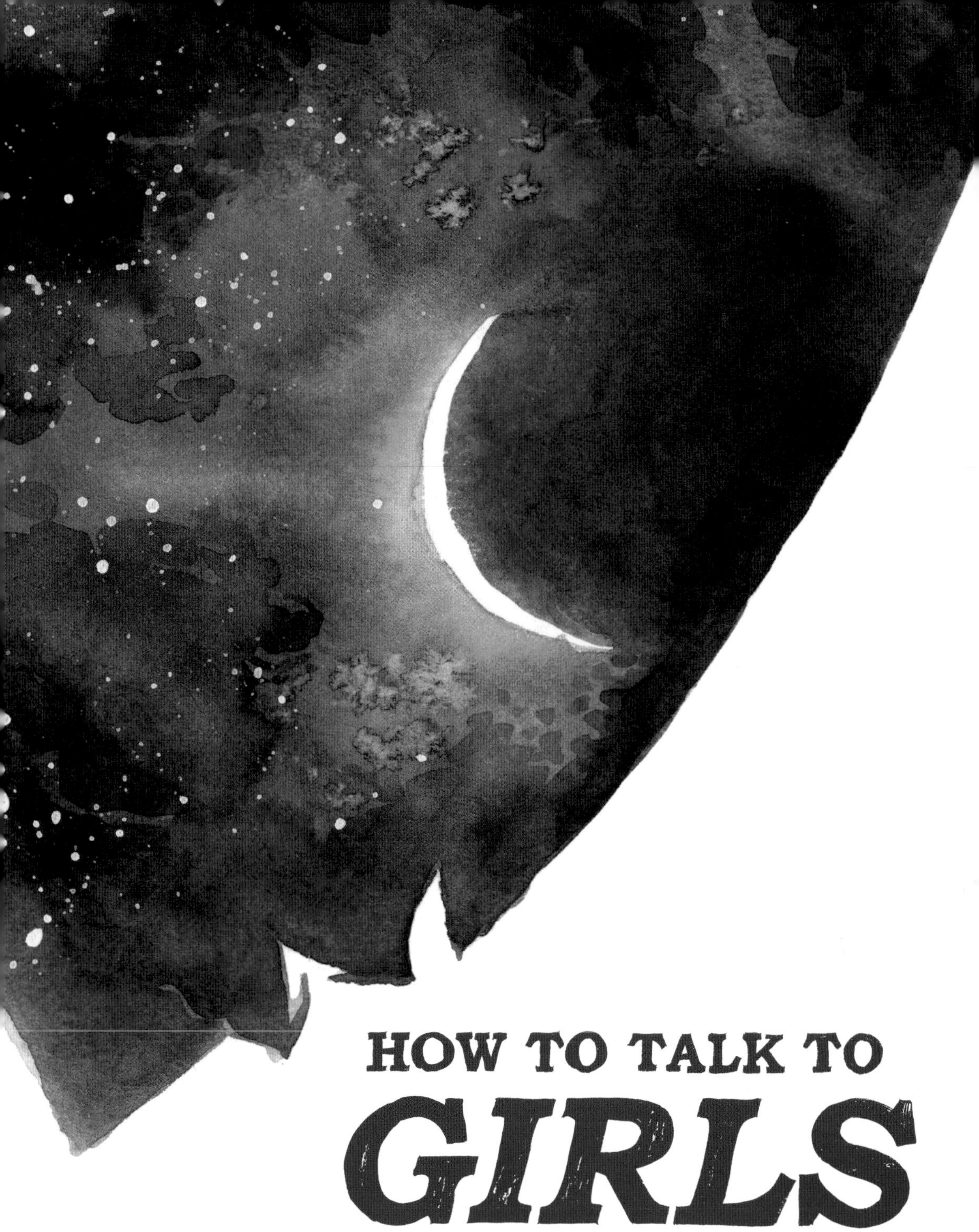

HOW TO TALK TO GIRLS AT PARTIES

by

Neil Gaiman

adaptation, art, & lettering by

Fábio Moon & Gabriel Bá

headline

Based on the short story 'How to Talk to Girls at Parties' by Neil Gaiman,
originally published in *Fragile Things* (Headline, 2006)

First published in the US in 2016 by Dark Horse Books

First published in Great Britain in 2016 by
HEADLINE PUBLISHING GROUP

1

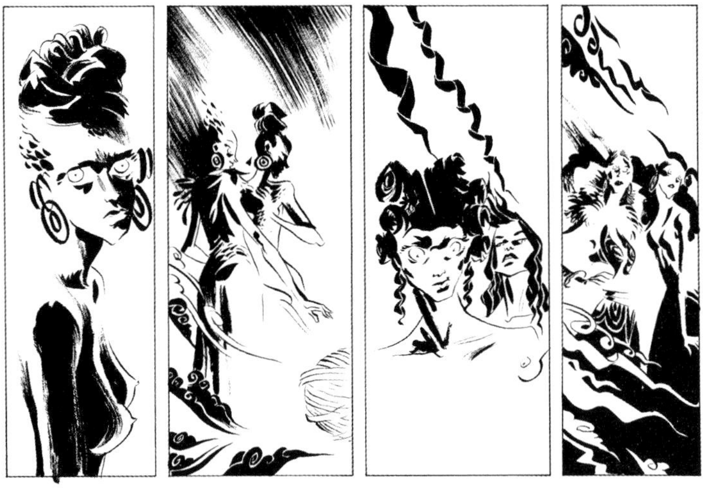

Cataloguing in Publication Data is available from the British Library

ISBN 978 1 4722 4248 8

Design by Cary Grazzini for Dark Horse Books

Printed and bound in Italy by Rotolito Lombarda S.p.A.

Headline's policy is to use papers that are natural, renewable and recyclable products and made from wood grown in sustainable forests. The logging and manufacturing processes are expected to conform to the environmental regulations of the country of origin.

HEADLINE PUBLISHING GROUP
An Hachette UK Company
Carmelite House
50 Victoria Embankment
London EC4Y 0DZ

www.headline.co.uk
www.hachette.co.uk

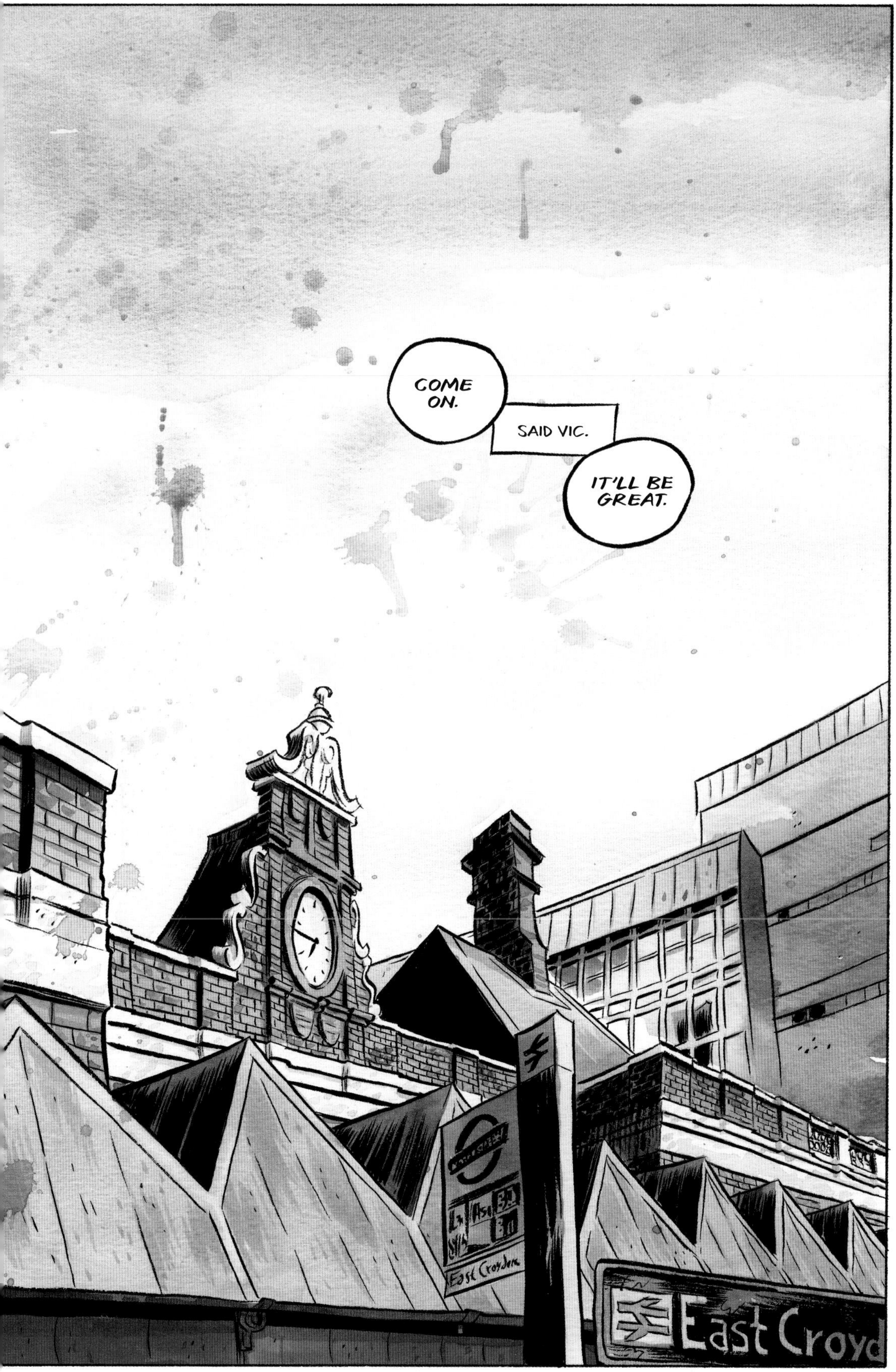
COME ON.
SAID VIC.
IT'LL BE GREAT.
East Croydon
East Croyd

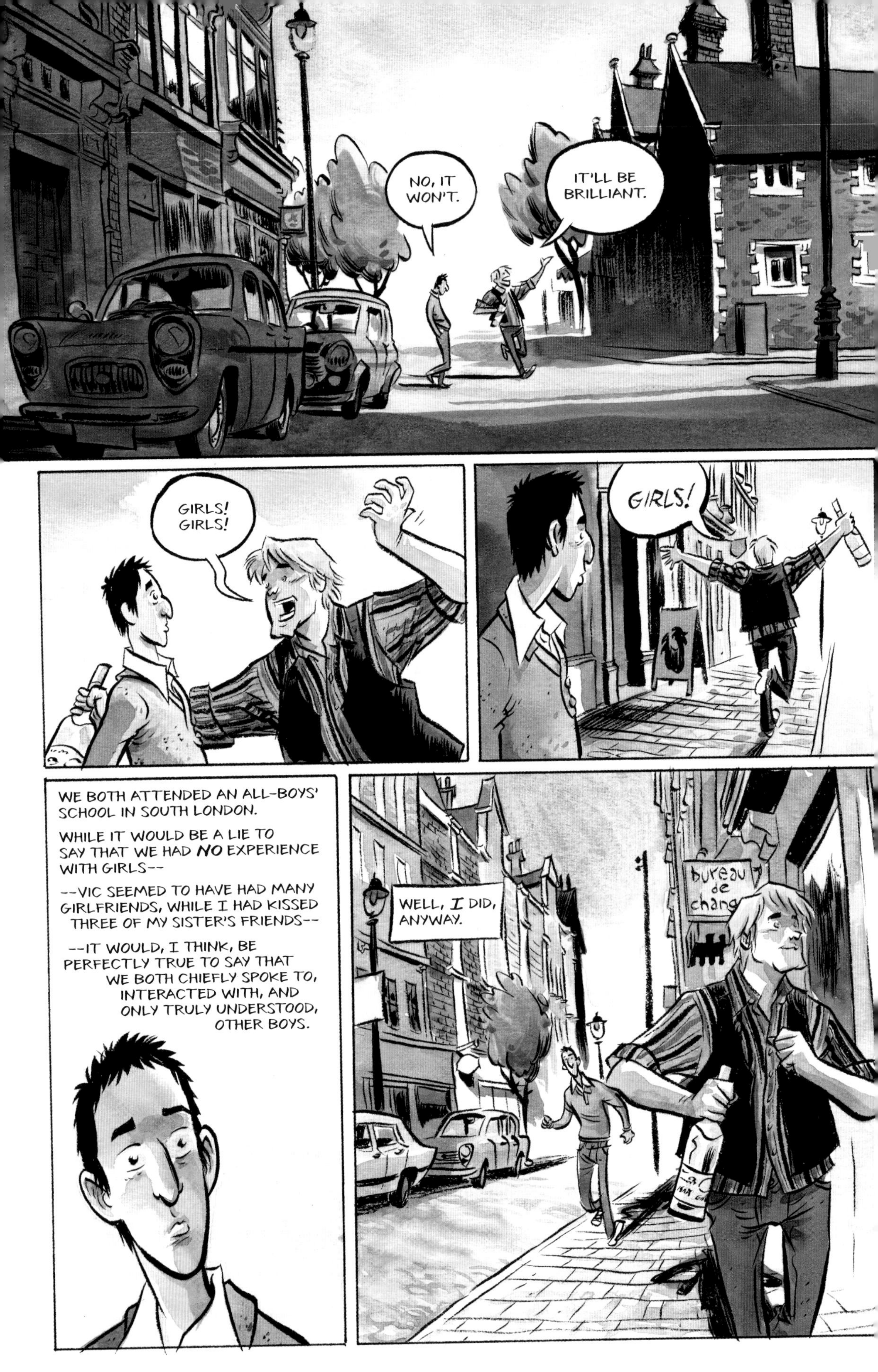
NO, IT WON'T.
IT'LL BE BRILLIANT.
GIRLS! GIRLS!
GIRLS!
WE BOTH ATTENDED AN ALL-BOYS' SCHOOL IN SOUTH LONDON.
WHILE IT WOULD BE A LIE TO SAY THAT WE HAD NO EXPERIENCE WITH GIRLS--
--VIC SEEMED TO HAVE HAD MANY GIRLFRIENDS, WHILE I HAD KISSED THREE OF MY SISTER'S FRIENDS--
--IT WOULD, I THINK, BE PERFECTLY TRUE TO SAY THAT WE BOTH CHIEFLY SPOKE TO, INTERACTED WITH, AND ONLY TRULY UNDERSTOOD, OTHER BOYS.
WELL, I DID, ANYWAY.
bureau de chang

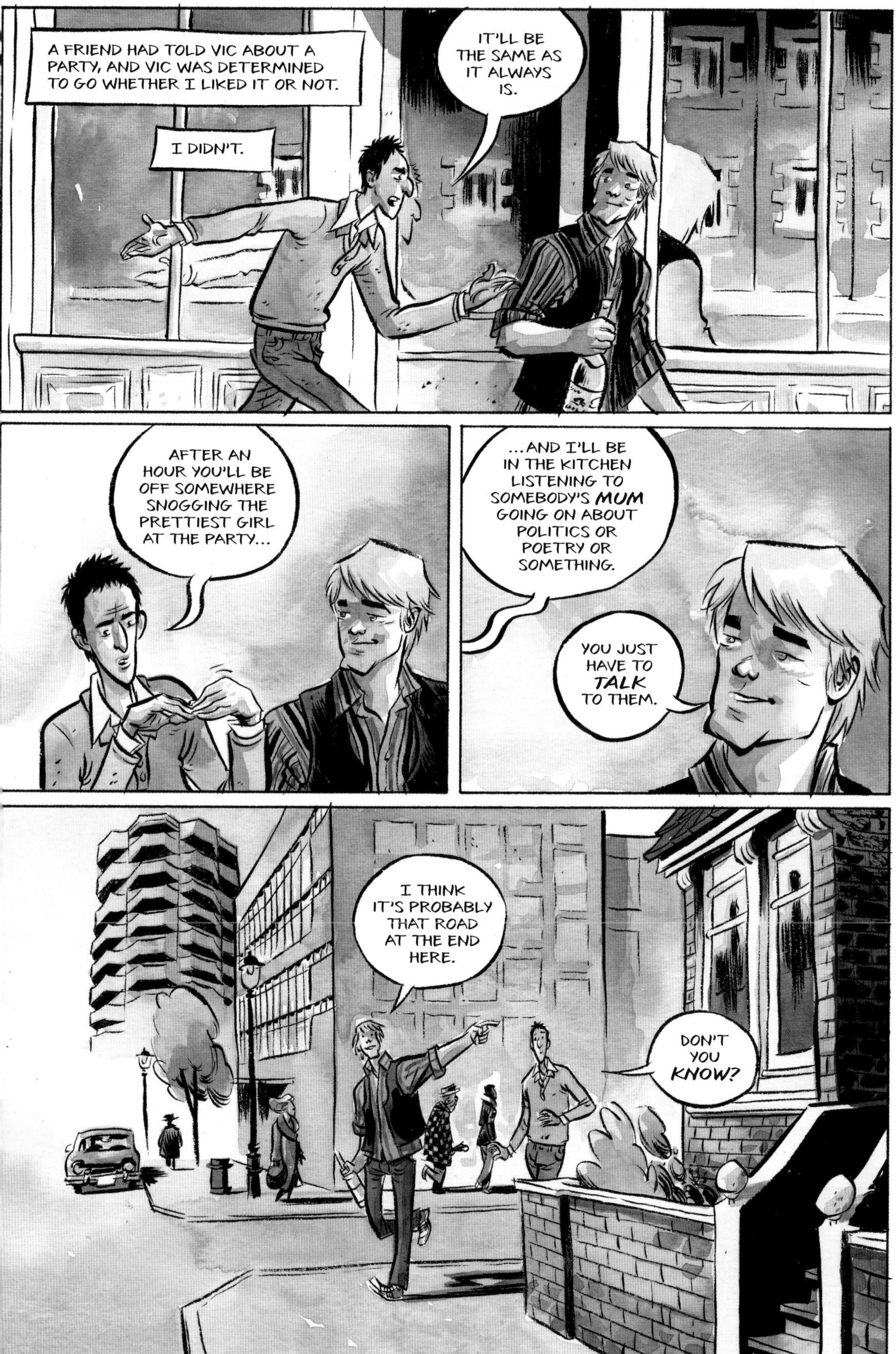
A FRIEND HAD TOLD VIC ABOUT A PARTY, AND VIC WAS DETERMINED TO GO WHETHER I LIKED IT OR NOT.
I DIDN'T.
IT'LL BE THE SAME AS IT ALWAYS IS.
AFTER AN HOUR YOU'LL BE OFF SOMEWHERE SNOGGING THE PRETTIEST GIRL AT THE PARTY...
...AND I'LL BE IN THE KITCHEN LISTENING TO SOMEBODY'S MUM GOING ON ABOUT POLITICS OR POETRY OR SOMETHING.
YOU JUST HAVE TO TALK TO THEM.
I THINK IT'S PROBABLY THAT ROAD AT THE END HERE.
DON'T YOU KNOW?

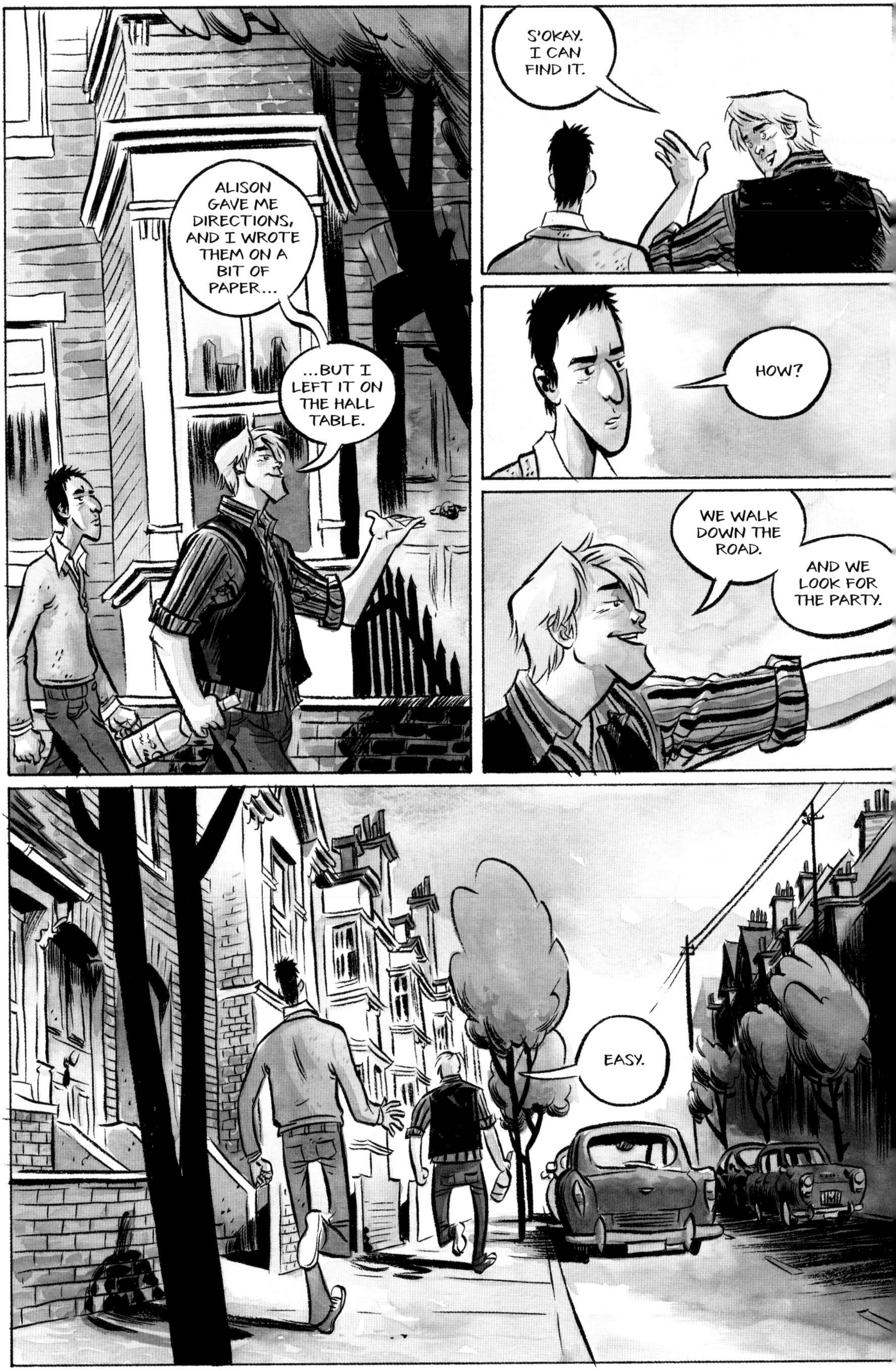
ALISON GAVE ME DIRECTIONS, AND I WROTE THEM ON A BIT OF PAPER...
...BUT I LEFT IT ON THE HALL TABLE.
S'OKAY. I CAN FIND IT.
HOW?
WE WALK DOWN THE ROAD.
AND WE LOOK FOR THE PARTY.
EASY.

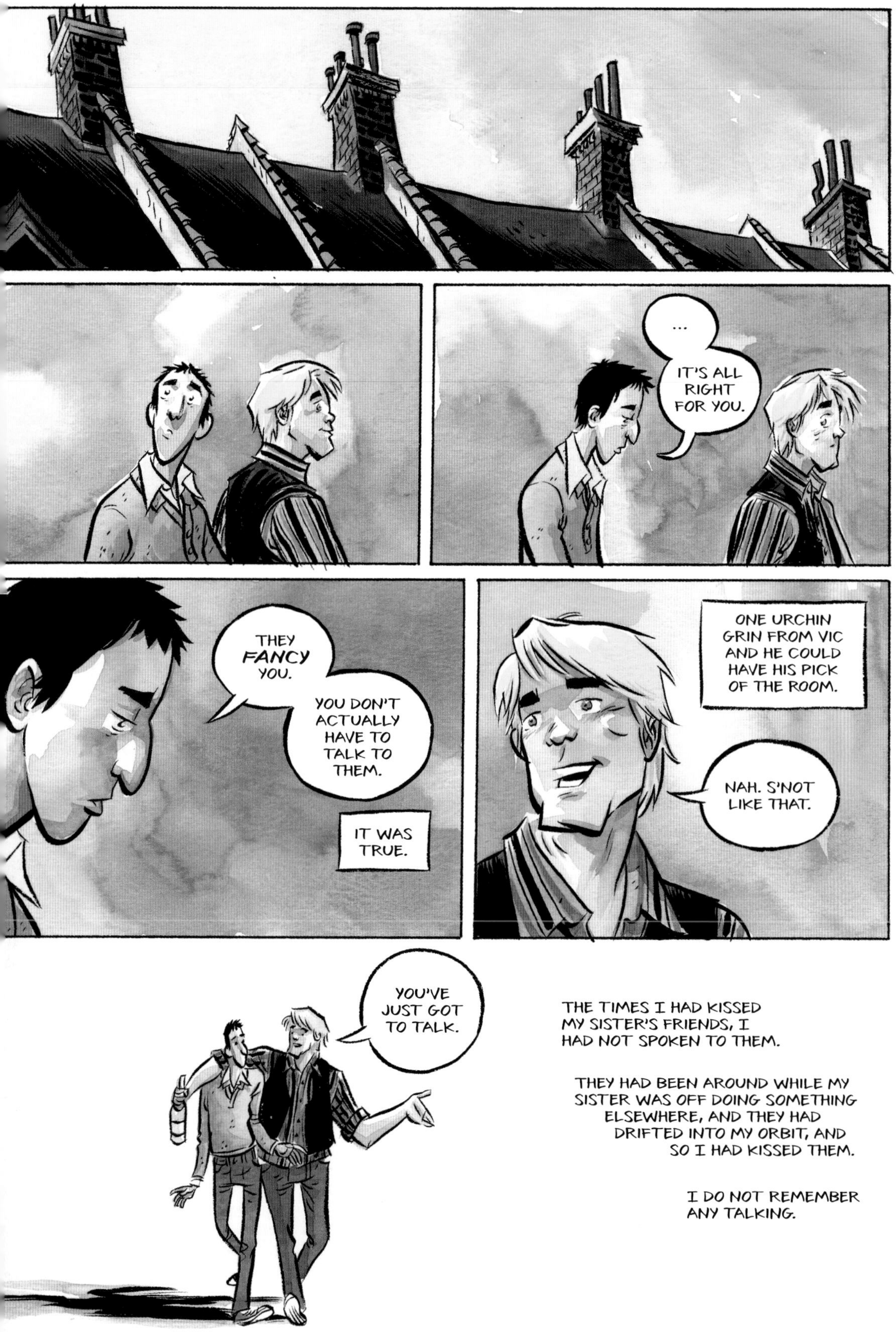
...
IT'S ALL RIGHT FOR YOU.
THEY FANCY YOU.
YOU DON'T ACTUALLY HAVE TO TALK TO THEM.
IT WAS TRUE.
ONE URCHIN GRIN FROM VIC AND HE COULD HAVE HIS PICK OF THE ROOM.
NAH. S'NOT LIKE THAT.
YOU'VE JUST GOT TO TALK.
THE TIMES I HAD KISSED MY SISTER'S FRIENDS, I HAD NOT SPOKEN TO THEM.
THEY HAD BEEN AROUND WHILE MY SISTER WAS OFF DOING SOMETHING ELSEWHERE, AND THEY HAD DRIFTED INTO MY ORBIT, AND SO I HAD KISSED THEM.
I DO NOT REMEMBER ANY TALKING.

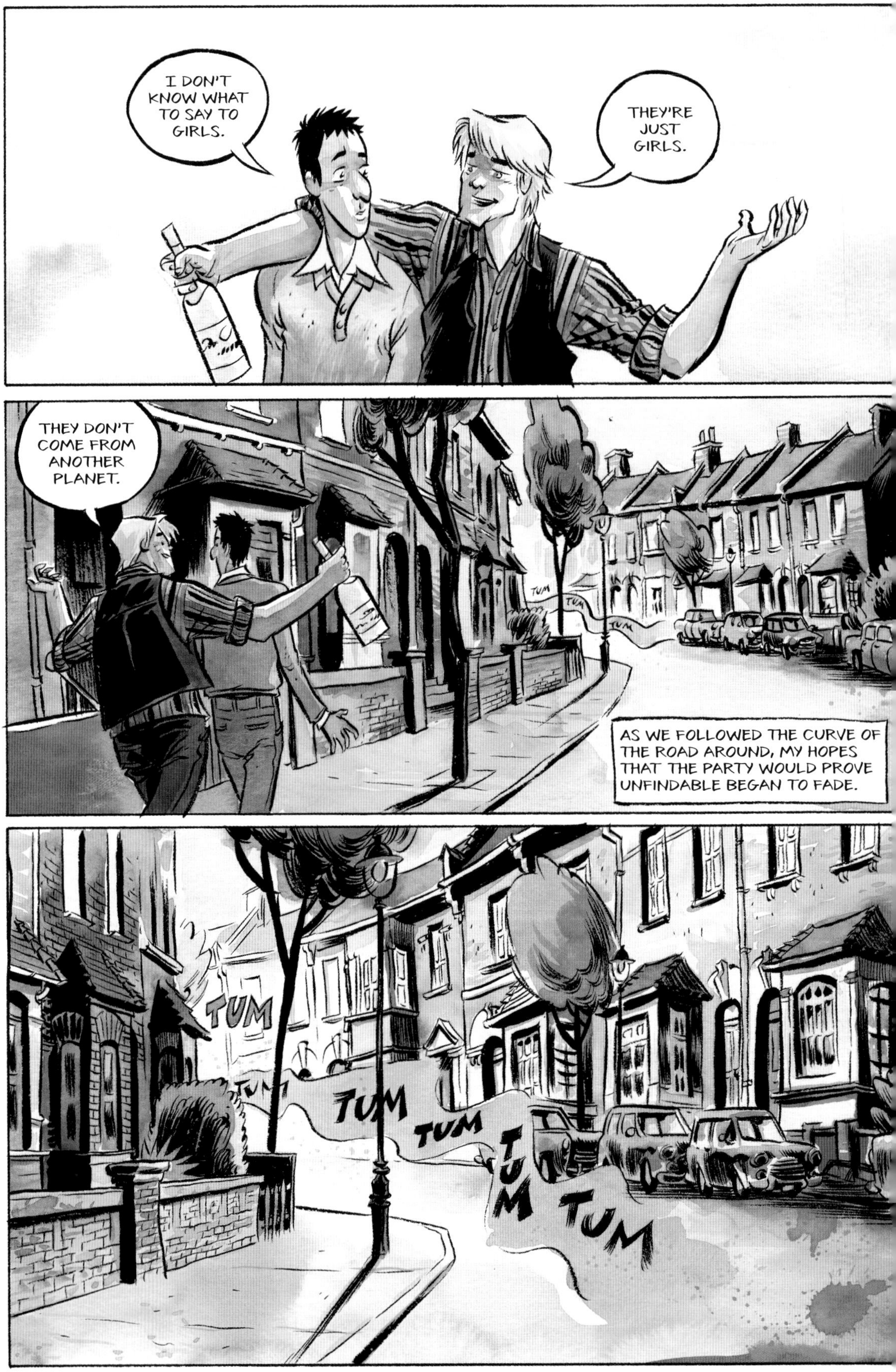
I DON'T KNOW WHAT TO SAY TO GIRLS.
THEY'RE JUST GIRLS.
THEY DON'T COME FROM ANOTHER PLANET.
TUM
TUM
TUM
AS WE FOLLOWED THE CURVE OF THE ROAD AROUND, MY HOPES THAT THE PARTY WOULD PROVE UNFINDABLE BEGAN TO FADE.
TUM
TUM
TUM
TUM
TUM
TUM
TUM

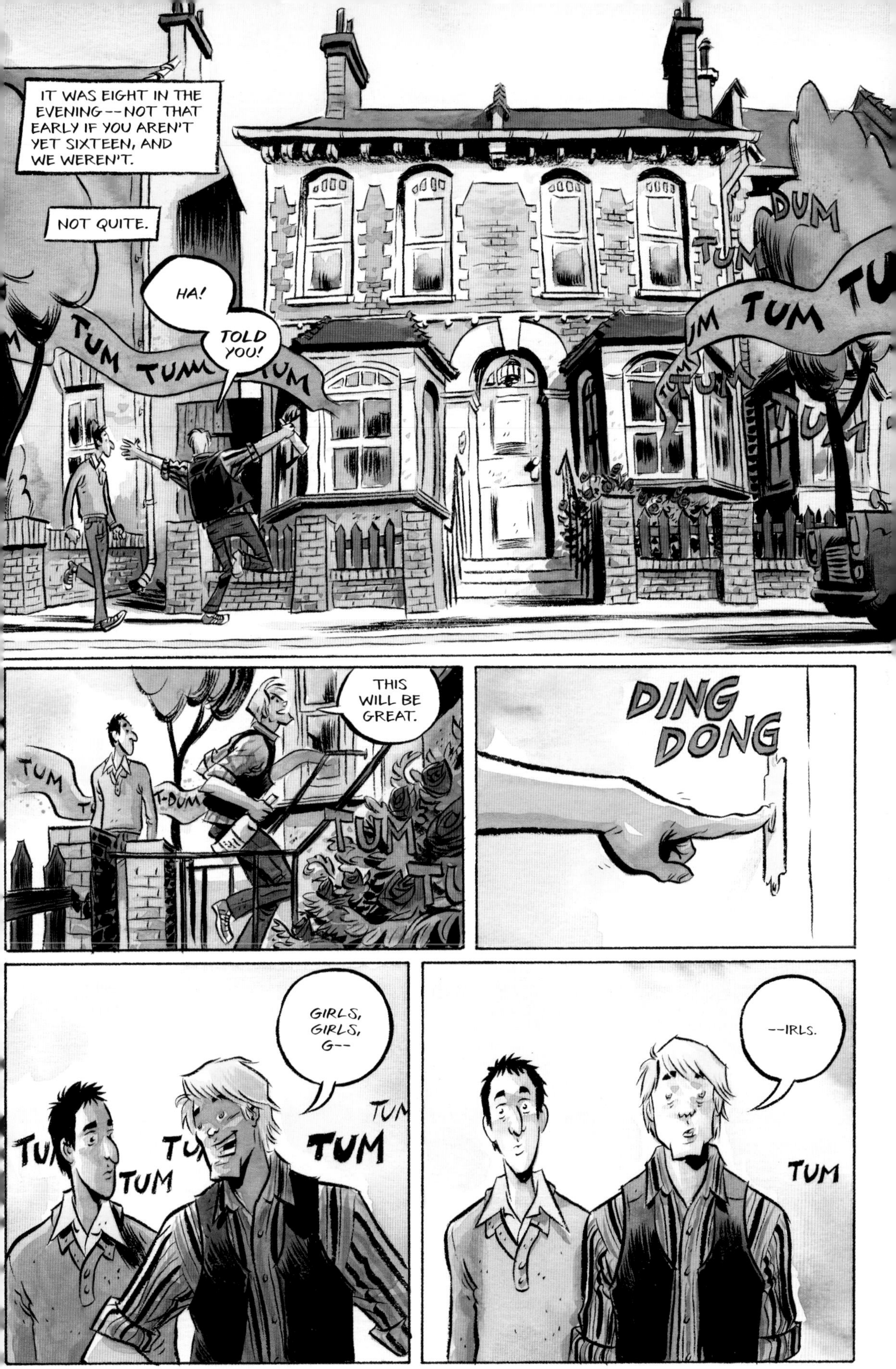
IT WAS EIGHT IN THE EVENING--NOT THAT EARLY IF YOU AREN'T YET SIXTEEN, AND WE WEREN'T.
NOT QUITE.
DUM
TUM
TUM TUM
HA!
TOLD YOU!
TUM TUM TUM
THIS WILL BE GREAT.
TUM
T-DUM
TUM
DING DONG
GIRLS, GIRLS, G--
TUM
TUM
TUM
TUM
--IRLS.
TUM

I COULD NOT HAVE TOLD YOU HOW OLD SHE WAS, WHICH WAS ONE OF THE THINGS ABOUT GIRLS I HAD BEGUN TO HATE.

WHEN YOU START OUT AS KIDS, YOU'RE JUST BOYS AND GIRLS, GOING THROUGH TIME AT THE SAME SPEED.

AND THEN ONE DAY THERE'S A LURCH AND THE GIRLS JUST SORT OF SPRINT OFF INTO THE FUTURE AHEAD OF YOU...

...AND THEY KNOW ALL ABOUT EVERYTHING, AND THEY HAVE PERIODS AND BREASTS AND MAKEUP AND GOD-ONLY-KNEW-WHAT-ELSE...

...FOR I CERTAINLY DIDN'T.

BIOLOGY DIAGRAMS WERE NO SUBSTITUTE FOR BEING, IN A VERY REAL SENSE, YOUNG ADULTS.

AND THE GIRLS OF OUR AGE WERE.

VIC AND I WEREN'T.

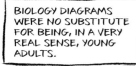

I WAS BEGINNING TO SUSPECT THAT, EVEN WHEN I STARTED NEEDING TO SHAVE EVERY DAY, I WOULD STILL BE WAY BEHIND.

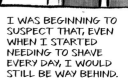

HELLO?

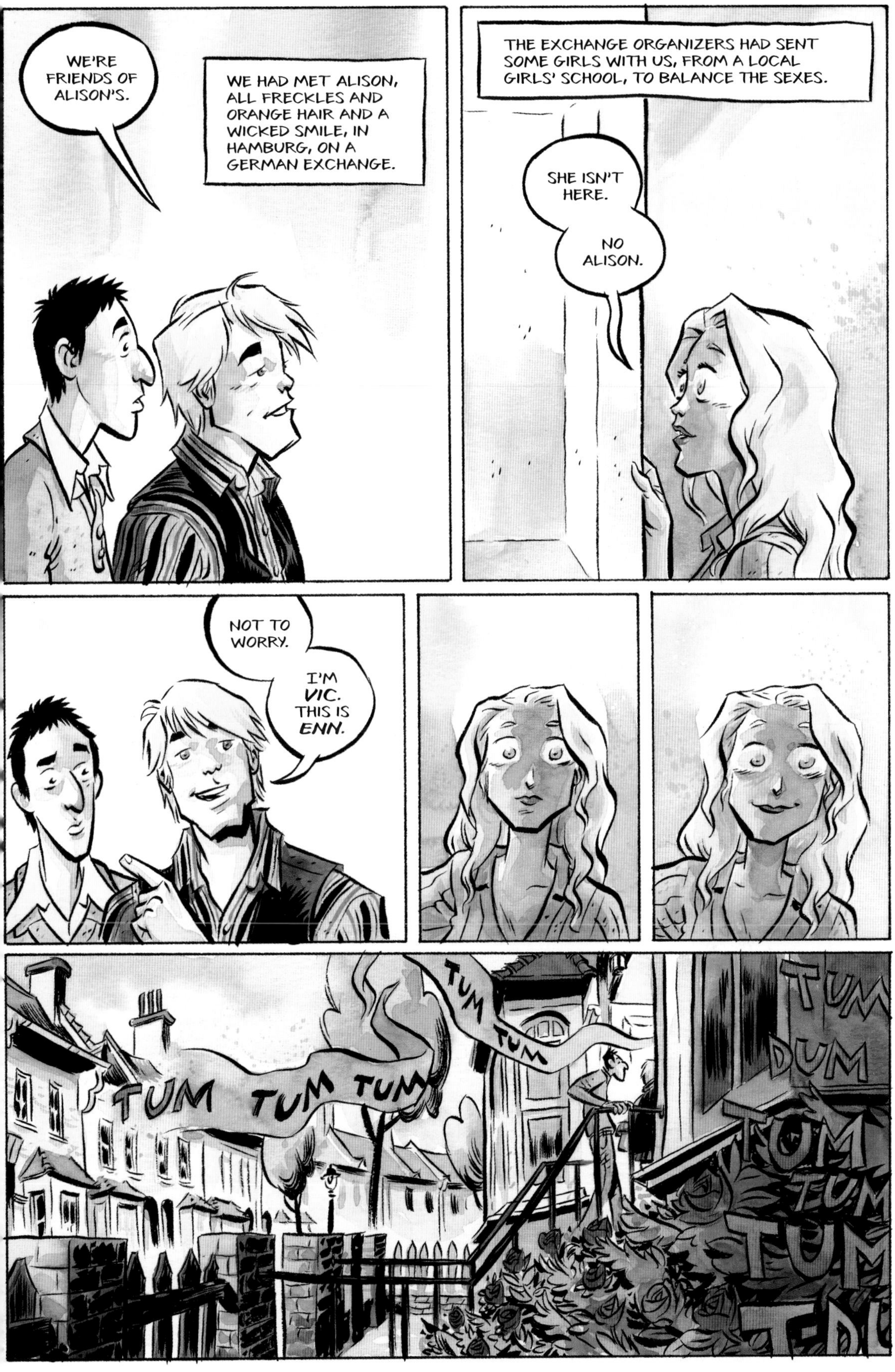
WE'RE FRIENDS OF ALISON'S.
WE HAD MET ALISON, ALL FRECKLES AND ORANGE HAIR AND A WICKED SMILE, IN HAMBURG, ON A GERMAN EXCHANGE.
THE EXCHANGE ORGANIZERS HAD SENT SOME GIRLS WITH US, FROM A LOCAL GIRLS' SCHOOL, TO BALANCE THE SEXES.
SHE ISN'T HERE.
NO ALISON.
NOT TO WORRY.
I'M VIC. THIS IS ENN.
TUM TUM TUM
TUM TUM
TUM
DUM
TUM
TUM
TUM

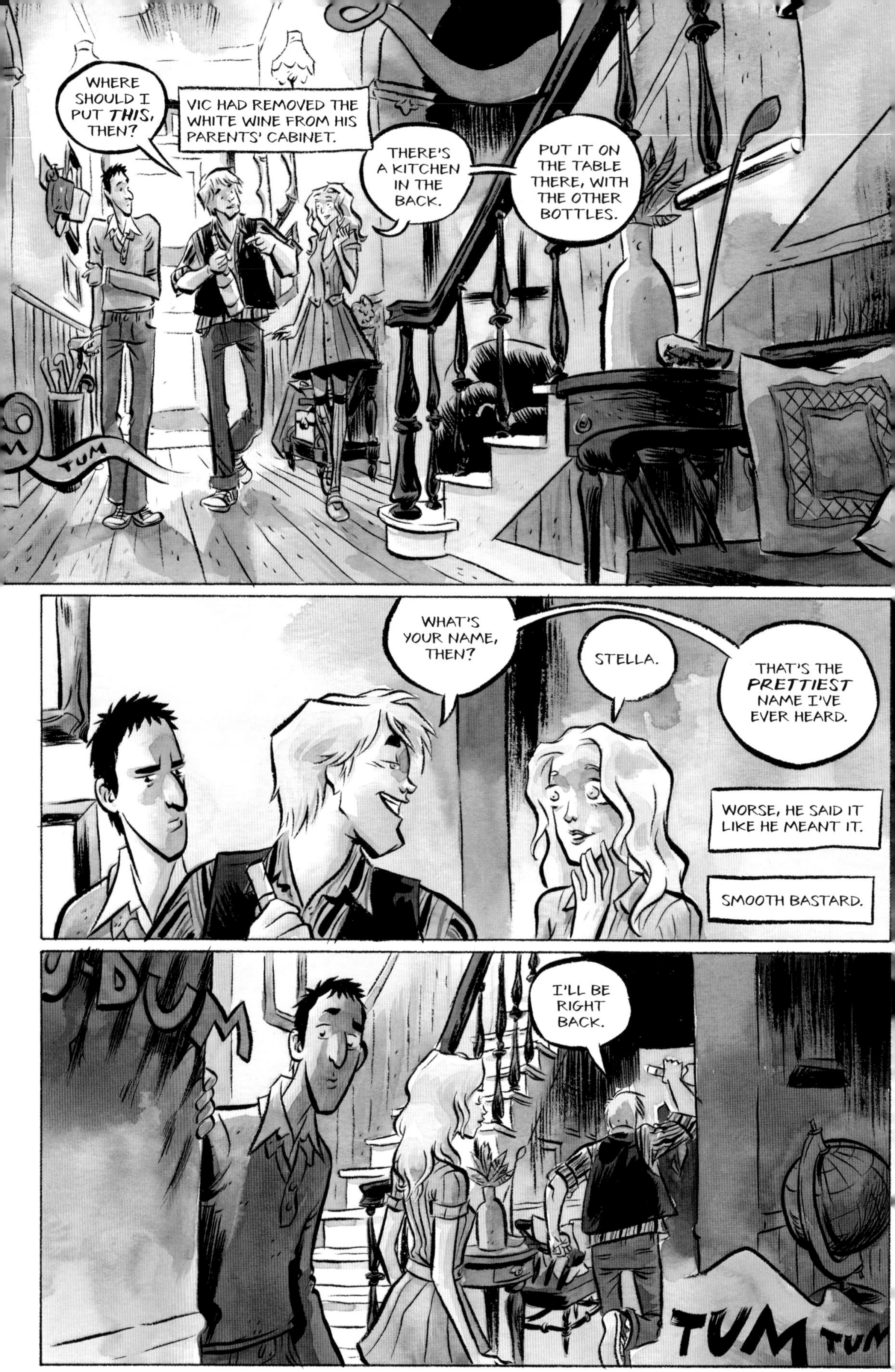
WHERE SHOULD I PUT *THIS*, THEN?
VIC HAD REMOVED THE WHITE WINE FROM HIS PARENTS' CABINET.
THERE'S A KITCHEN IN THE BACK.
PUT IT ON THE TABLE THERE, WITH THE OTHER BOTTLES.
TUM
WHAT'S YOUR NAME, THEN?
STELLA.
THAT'S THE *PRETTIEST* NAME I'VE EVER HEARD.
WORSE, HE SAID IT LIKE HE MEANT IT.
SMOOTH BASTARD.
I'LL BE RIGHT BACK.
TUM

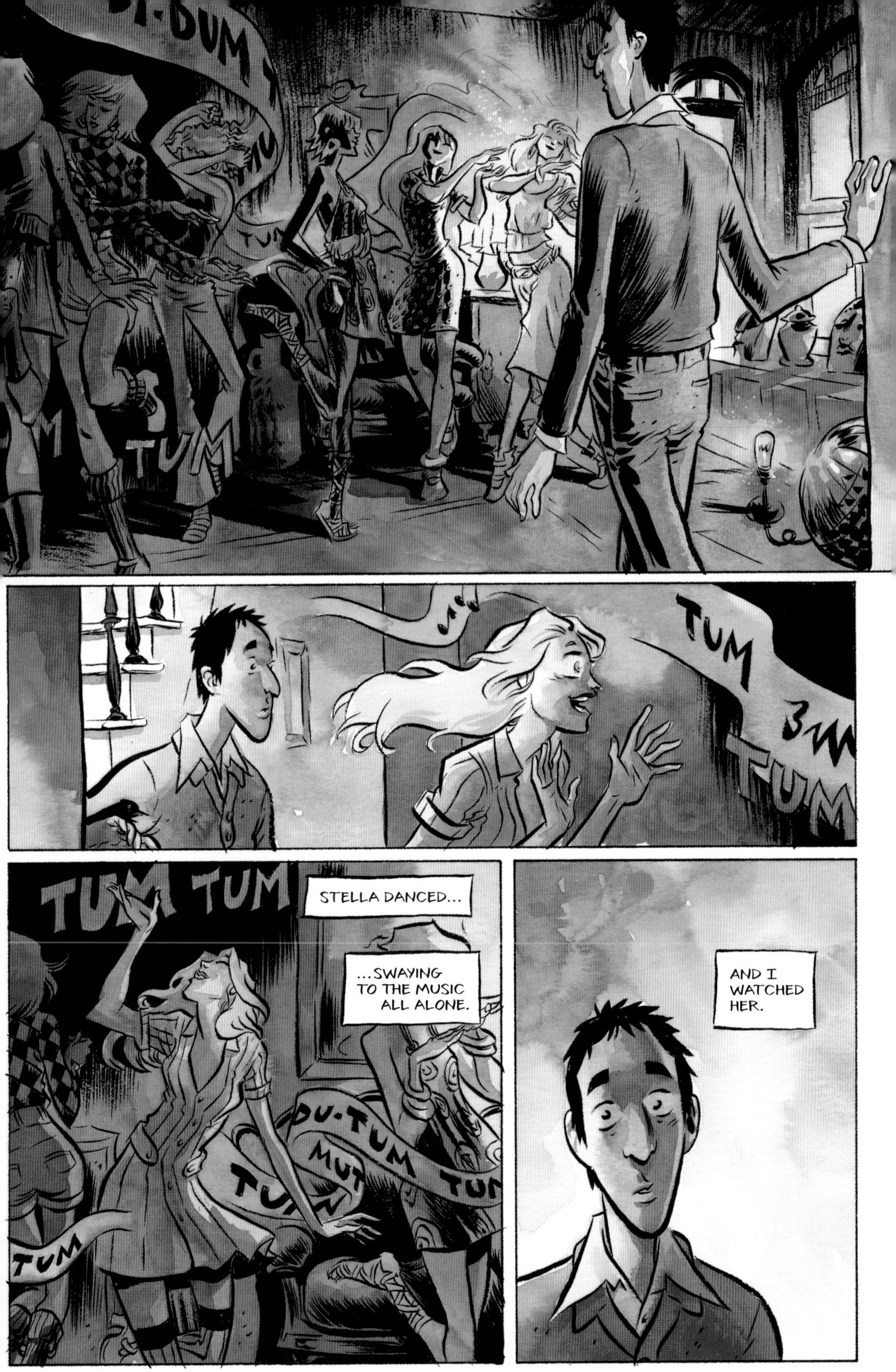
TUM
TUM
TUM
TUM TUM
STELLA DANCED...
...SWAYING
TO THE MUSIC
ALL ALONE.
DU-TUM
TUM
TUM
AND I
WATCHED
HER.

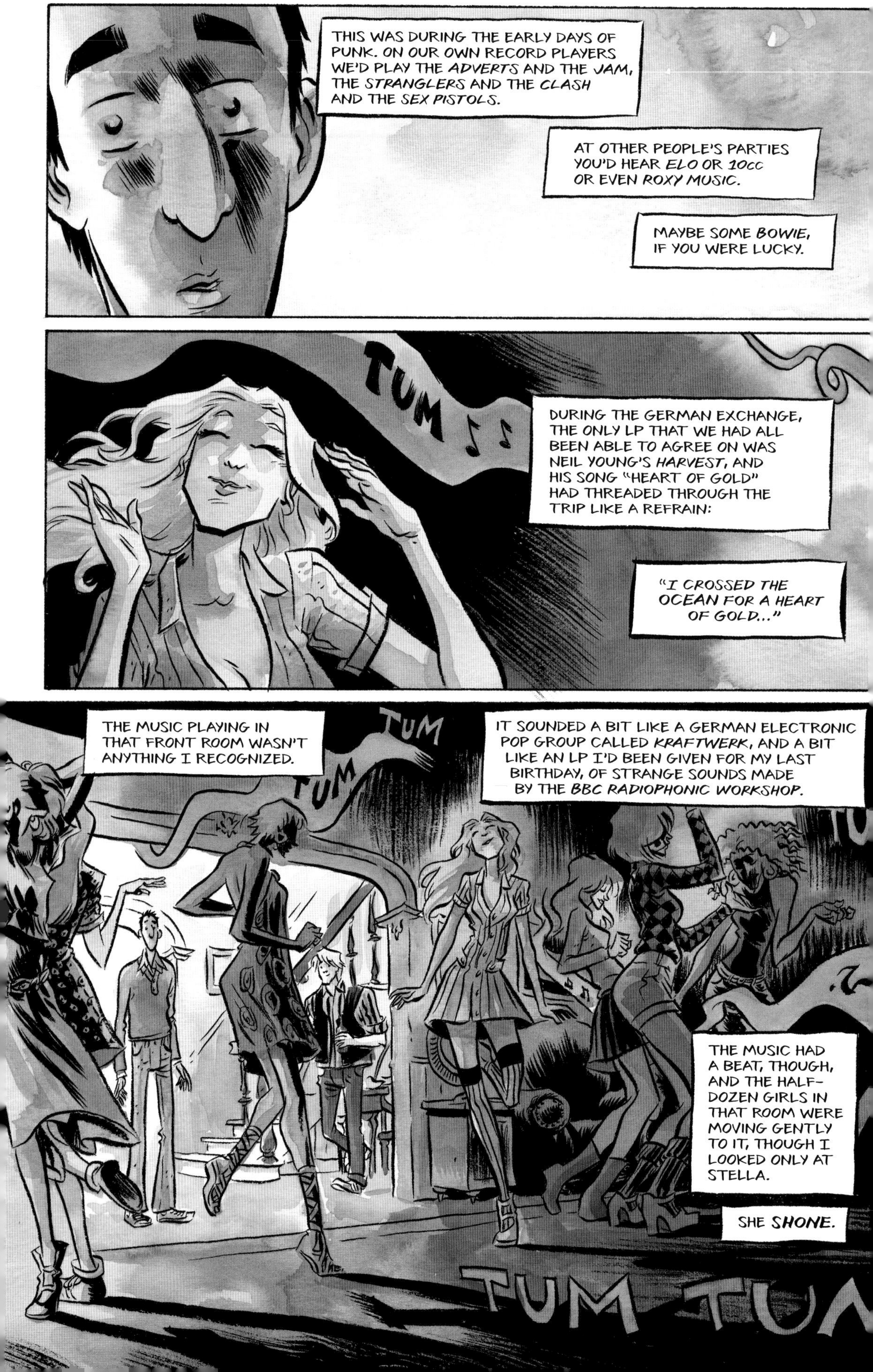
THIS WAS DURING THE EARLY DAYS OF PUNK. ON OUR OWN RECORD PLAYERS WE'D PLAY THE ADVERTS AND THE JAM, THE STRANGLERS AND THE CLASH AND THE SEX PISTOLS.
AT OTHER PEOPLE'S PARTIES YOU'D HEAR ELO OR 10cc OR EVEN ROXY MUSIC.
MAYBE SOME BOWIE, IF YOU WERE LUCKY.
TUM
DURING THE GERMAN EXCHANGE, THE ONLY LP THAT WE HAD ALL BEEN ABLE TO AGREE ON WAS NEIL YOUNG'S HARVEST, AND HIS SONG "HEART OF GOLD" HAD THREADED THROUGH THE TRIP LIKE A REFRAIN:
"I CROSSED THE OCEAN FOR A HEART OF GOLD..."
THE MUSIC PLAYING IN THAT FRONT ROOM WASN'T ANYTHING I RECOGNIZED.
TUM
TUM
IT SOUNDED A BIT LIKE A GERMAN ELECTRONIC POP GROUP CALLED KRAFTWERK, AND A BIT LIKE AN LP I'D BEEN GIVEN FOR MY LAST BIRTHDAY, OF STRANGE SOUNDS MADE BY THE BBC RADIOPHONIC WORKSHOP.
THE MUSIC HAD A BEAT, THOUGH, AND THE HALF-DOZEN GIRLS IN THAT ROOM WERE MOVING GENTLY TO IT, THOUGH I LOOKED ONLY AT STELLA.
SHE SHONE.
TUM TUM

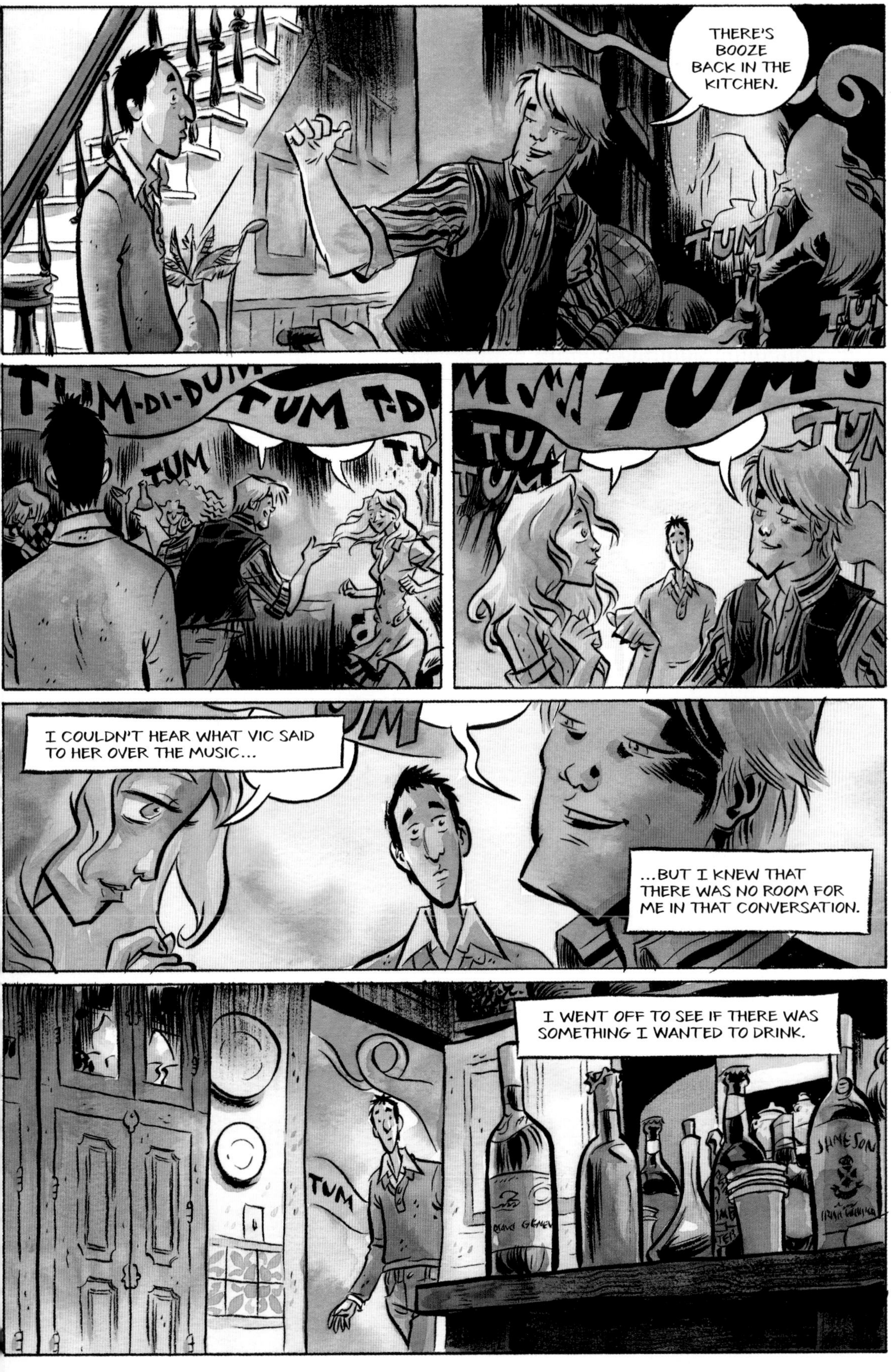
THERE'S BOOZE BACK IN THE KITCHEN.
TUM
TUM
TUM-DI-DUM TUM T-D
TUM
TUM
TUM
TUM
TUM
I COULDN'T HEAR WHAT VIC SAID TO HER OVER THE MUSIC...
...BUT I KNEW THAT THERE WAS NO ROOM FOR ME IN THAT CONVERSATION.
I WENT OFF TO SEE IF THERE WAS SOMETHING I WANTED TO DRINK.
TUM

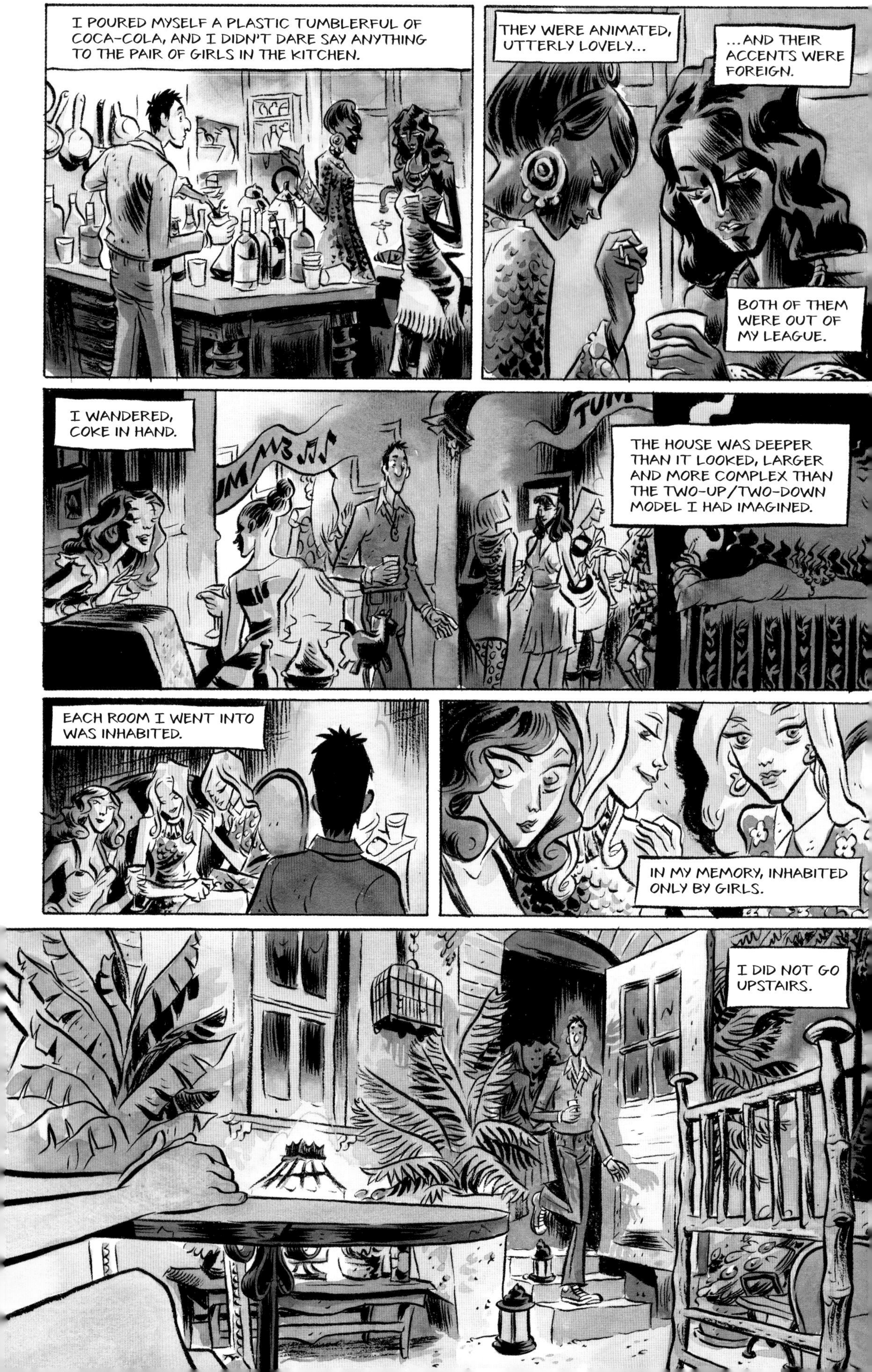
I POURED MYSELF A PLASTIC TUMBLERFUL OF COCA-COLA, AND I DIDN'T DARE SAY ANYTHING TO THE PAIR OF GIRLS IN THE KITCHEN.
THEY WERE ANIMATED, UTTERLY LOVELY...
...AND THEIR ACCENTS WERE FOREIGN.
BOTH OF THEM WERE OUT OF MY LEAGUE.
I WANDERED, COKE IN HAND.
THE HOUSE WAS DEEPER THAN IT LOOKED, LARGER AND MORE COMPLEX THAN THE TWO-UP/TWO-DOWN MODEL I HAD IMAGINED.
EACH ROOM I WENT INTO WAS INHABITED.
IN MY MEMORY, INHABITED ONLY BY GIRLS.
I DID NOT GO UPSTAIRS.

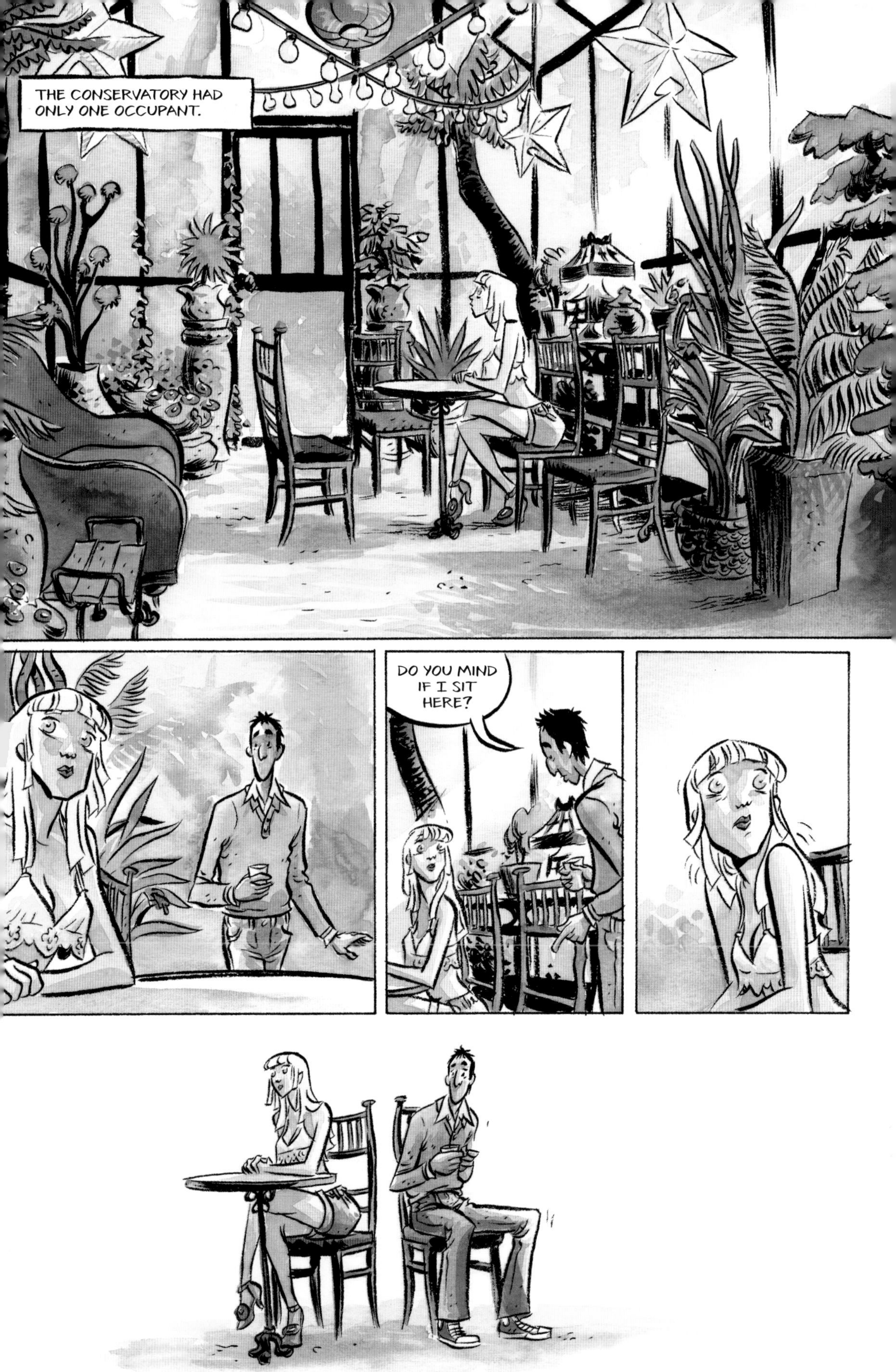
THE CONSERVATORY HAD ONLY ONE OCCUPANT.
DO YOU MIND IF I SIT HERE?

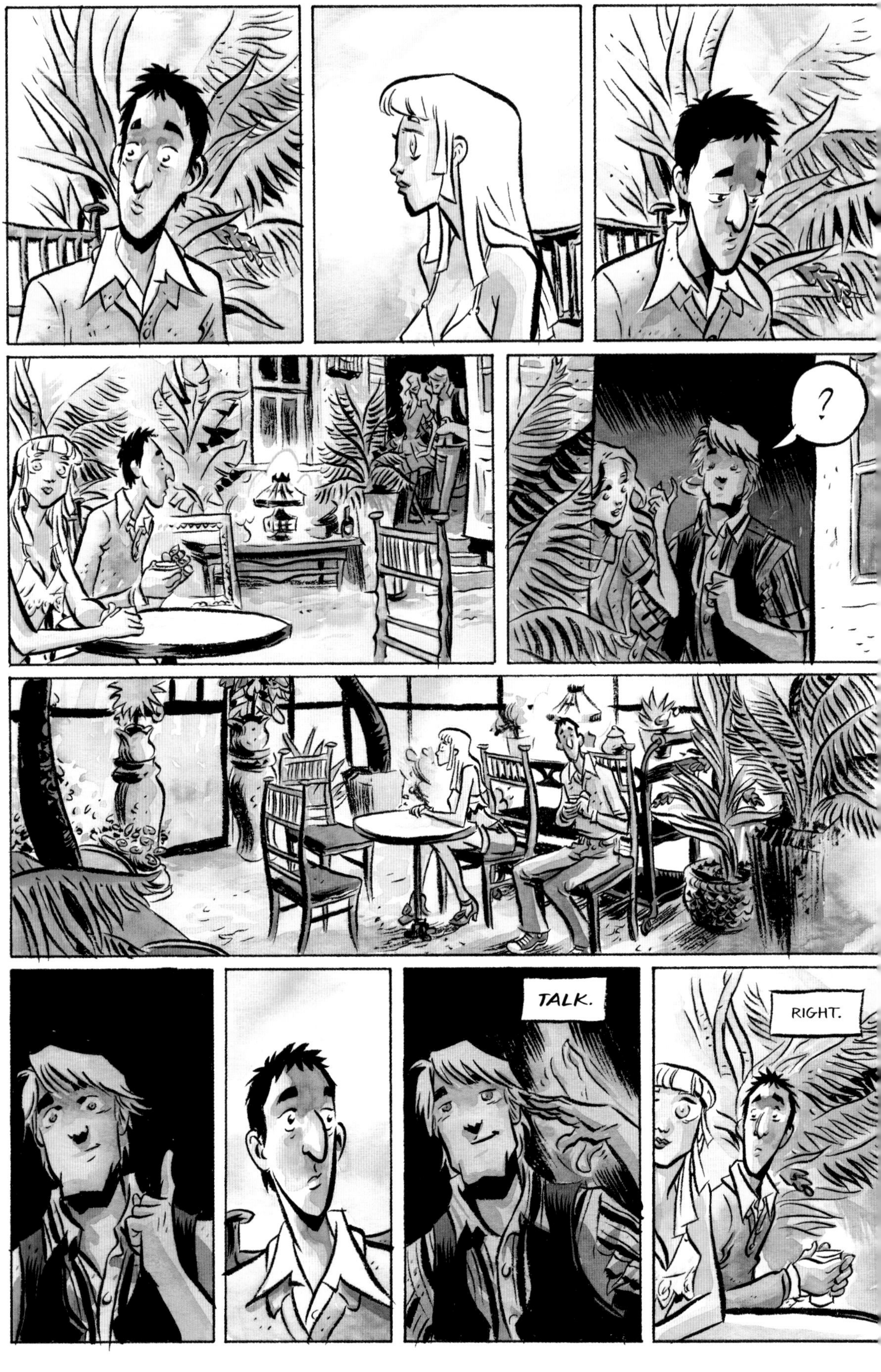
?
TALK.
RIGHT.

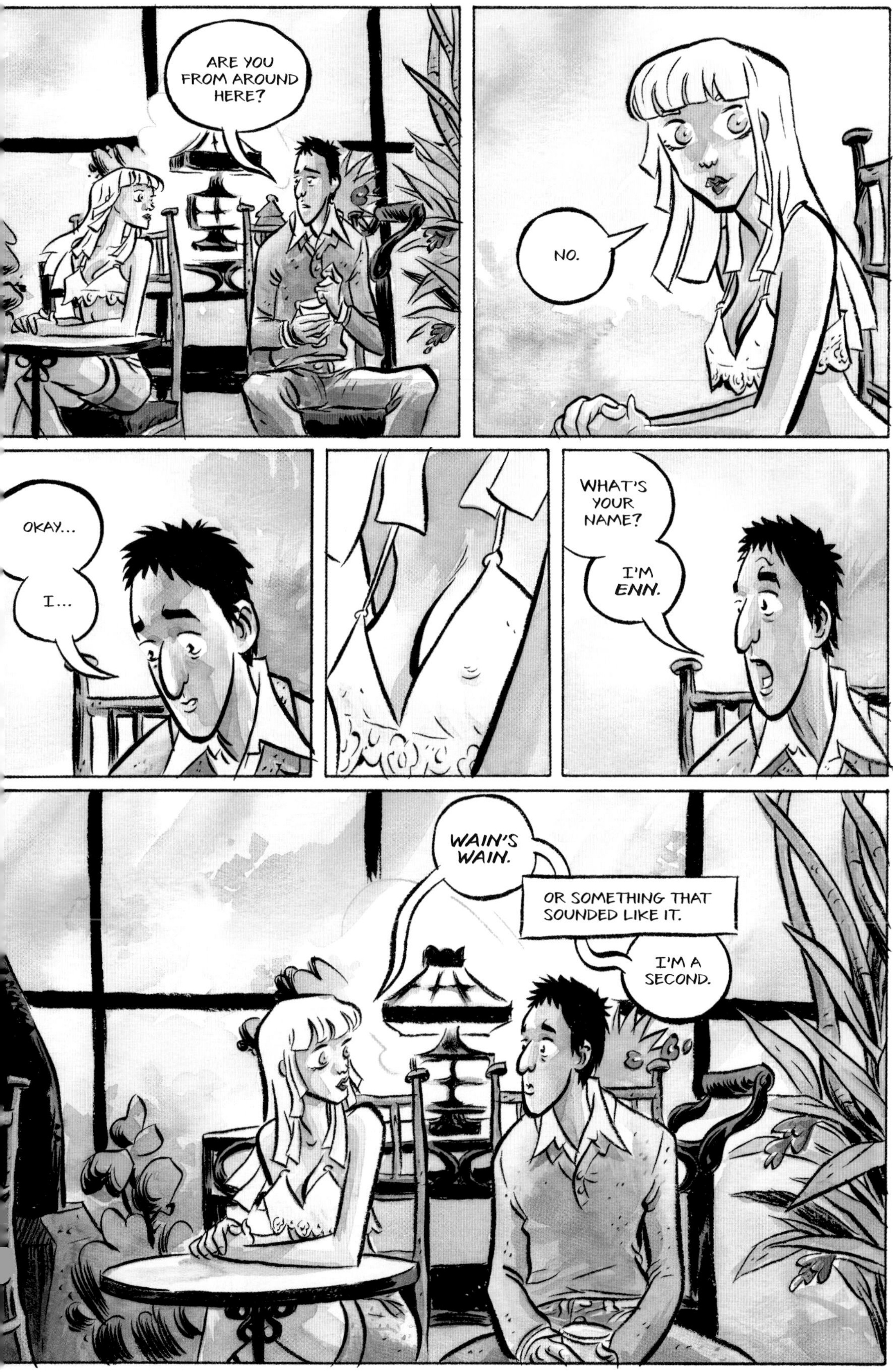
ARE YOU FROM AROUND HERE?
NO.
OKAY...
I...
WHAT'S YOUR NAME?
I'M ENN.
WAIN'S WAIN.
OR SOMETHING THAT SOUNDED LIKE IT.
I'M A SECOND.

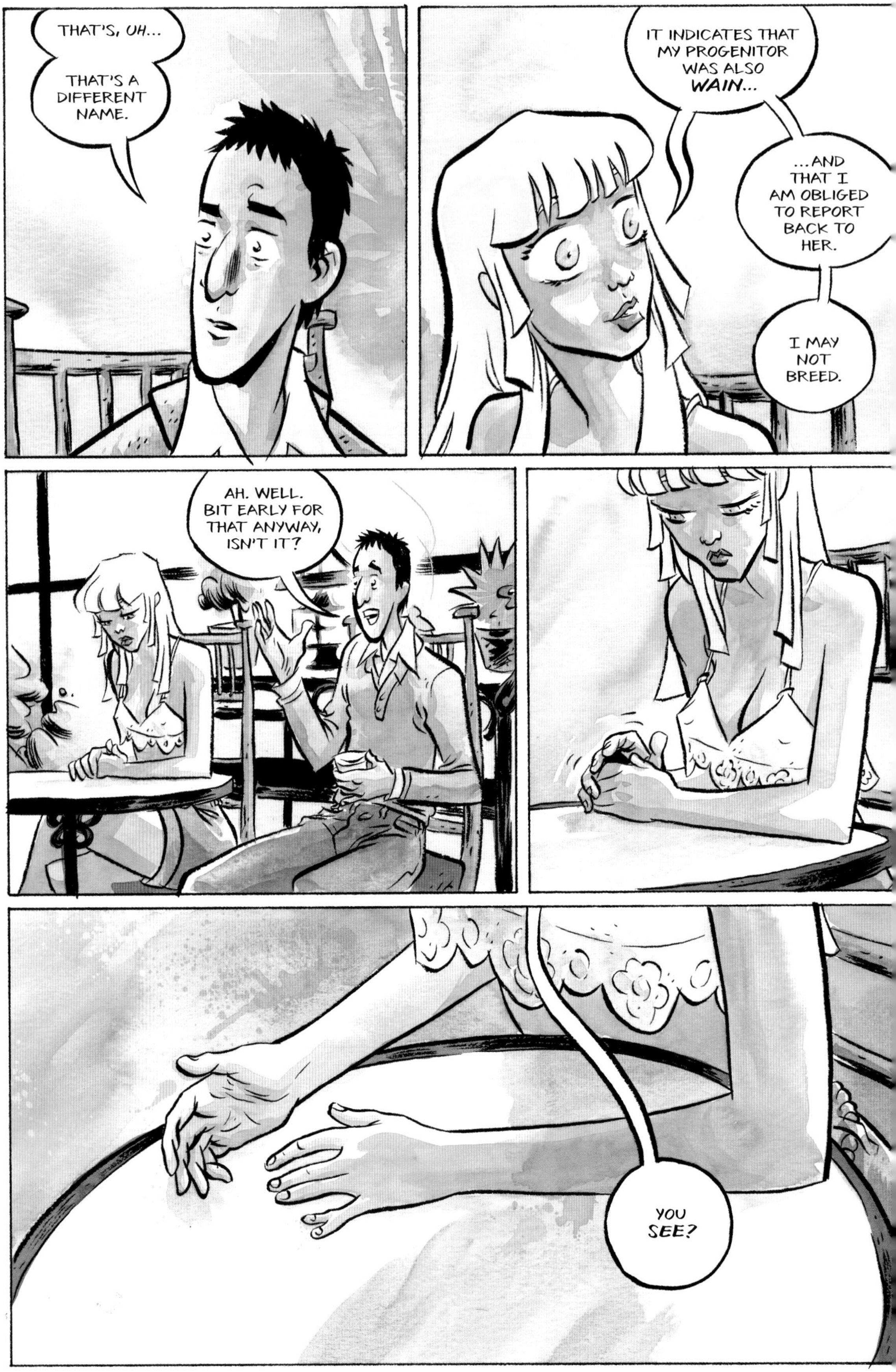
THAT'S, UH...
THAT'S A DIFFERENT NAME.
IT INDICATES THAT MY PROGENITOR WAS ALSO WAIN...
...AND THAT I AM OBLIGED TO REPORT BACK TO HER.
I MAY NOT BREED.
AH. WELL. BIT EARLY FOR THAT ANYWAY, ISN'T IT?
YOU SEE?

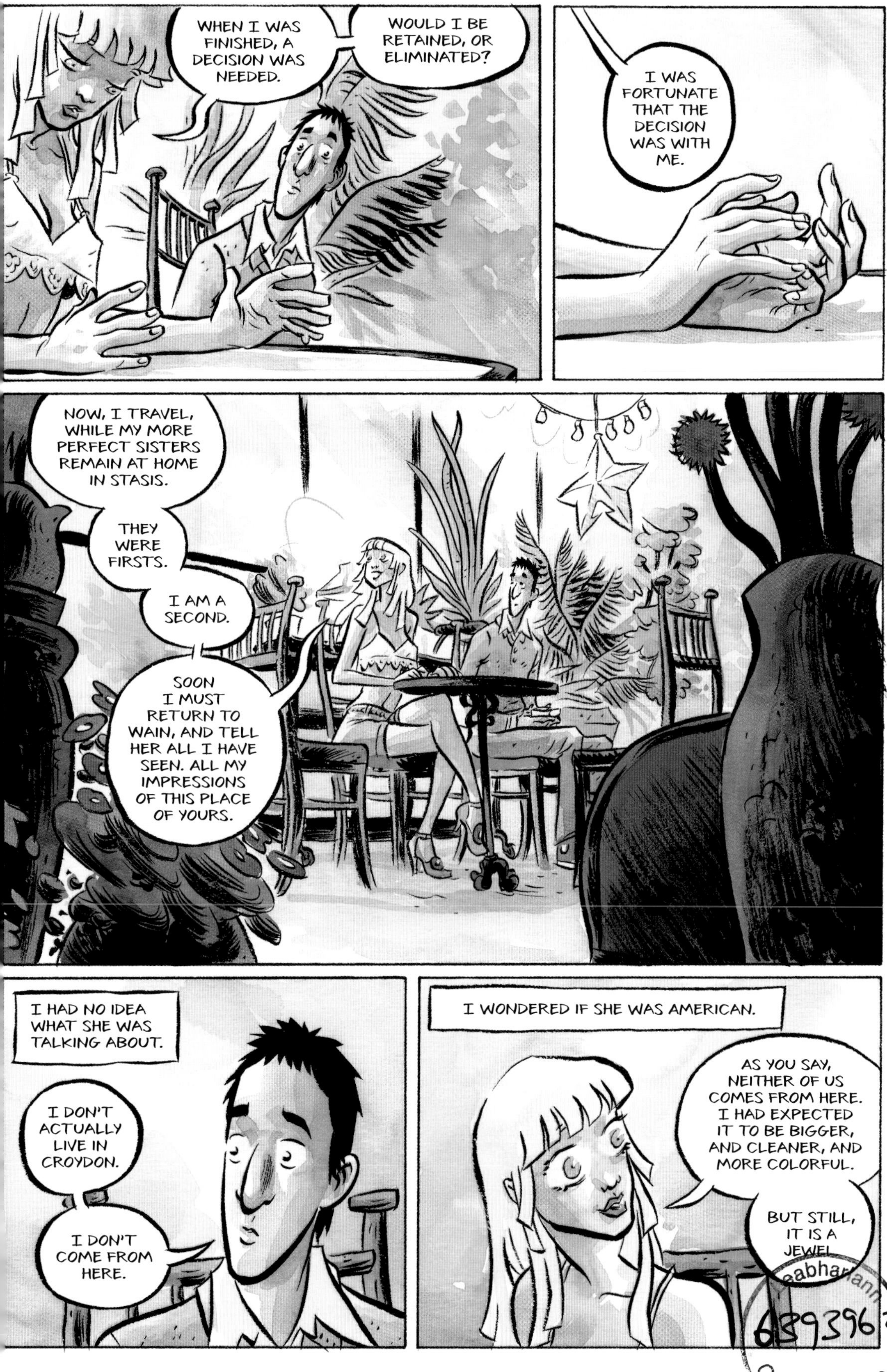
WHEN I WAS FINISHED, A DECISION WAS NEEDED.
WOULD I BE RETAINED, OR ELIMINATED?
I WAS FORTUNATE THAT THE DECISION WAS WITH ME.
NOW, I TRAVEL, WHILE MY MORE PERFECT SISTERS REMAIN AT HOME IN STASIS.
THEY WERE FIRSTS.
I AM A SECOND.
SOON I MUST RETURN TO WAIN, AND TELL HER ALL I HAVE SEEN. ALL MY IMPRESSIONS OF THIS PLACE OF YOURS.
I HAD NO IDEA WHAT SHE WAS TALKING ABOUT.
I DON'T ACTUALLY LIVE IN CROYDON.
I DON'T COME FROM HERE.
I WONDERED IF SHE WAS AMERICAN.
AS YOU SAY, NEITHER OF US COMES FROM HERE. I HAD EXPECTED IT TO BE BIGGER, AND CLEANER, AND MORE COLORFUL.
BUT STILL, IT IS A JEWEL

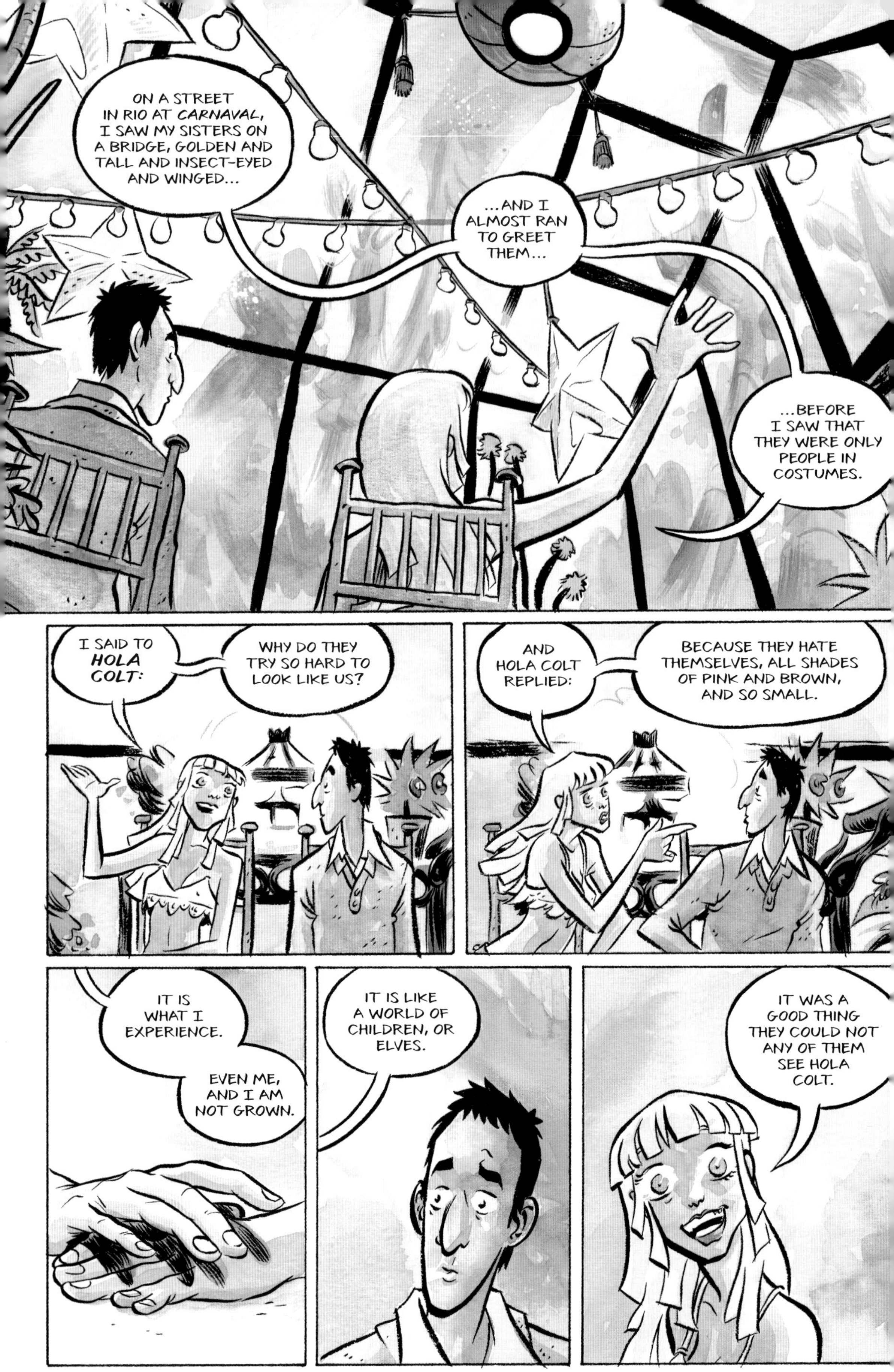
ON A STREET IN RIO AT CARNAVAL, I SAW MY SISTERS ON A BRIDGE, GOLDEN AND TALL AND INSECT-EYED AND WINGED...
...AND I ALMOST RAN TO GREET THEM...
...BEFORE I SAW THAT THEY WERE ONLY PEOPLE IN COSTUMES.
I SAID TO HOLA COLT:
WHY DO THEY TRY SO HARD TO LOOK LIKE US?
AND HOLA COLT REPLIED:
BECAUSE THEY HATE THEMSELVES, ALL SHADES OF PINK AND BROWN, AND SO SMALL.
IT IS WHAT I EXPERIENCE.
EVEN ME, AND I AM NOT GROWN.
IT IS LIKE A WORLD OF CHILDREN, OR ELVES.
IT WAS A GOOD THING THEY COULD NOT ANY OF THEM SEE HOLA COLT.

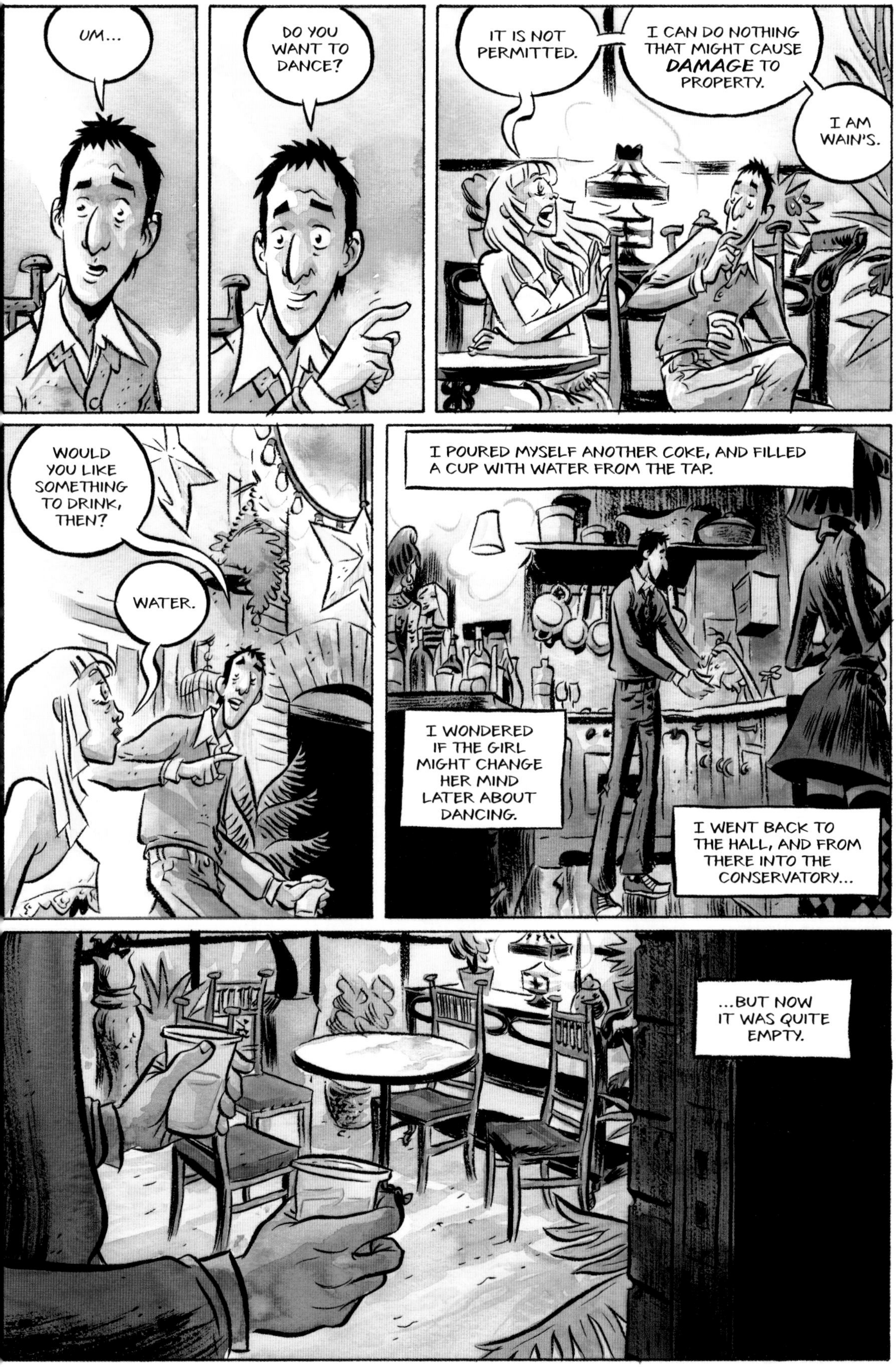
UM...
DO YOU WANT TO DANCE?
IT IS NOT PERMITTED.
I CAN DO NOTHING THAT MIGHT CAUSE DAMAGE TO PROPERTY.
I AM WAIN'S.
WOULD YOU LIKE SOMETHING TO DRINK, THEN?
WATER.
I POURED MYSELF ANOTHER COKE, AND FILLED A CUP WITH WATER FROM THE TAP.
I WONDERED IF THE GIRL MIGHT CHANGE HER MIND LATER ABOUT DANCING.
I WENT BACK TO THE HALL, AND FROM THERE INTO THE CONSERVATORY...
...BUT NOW IT WAS QUITE EMPTY.

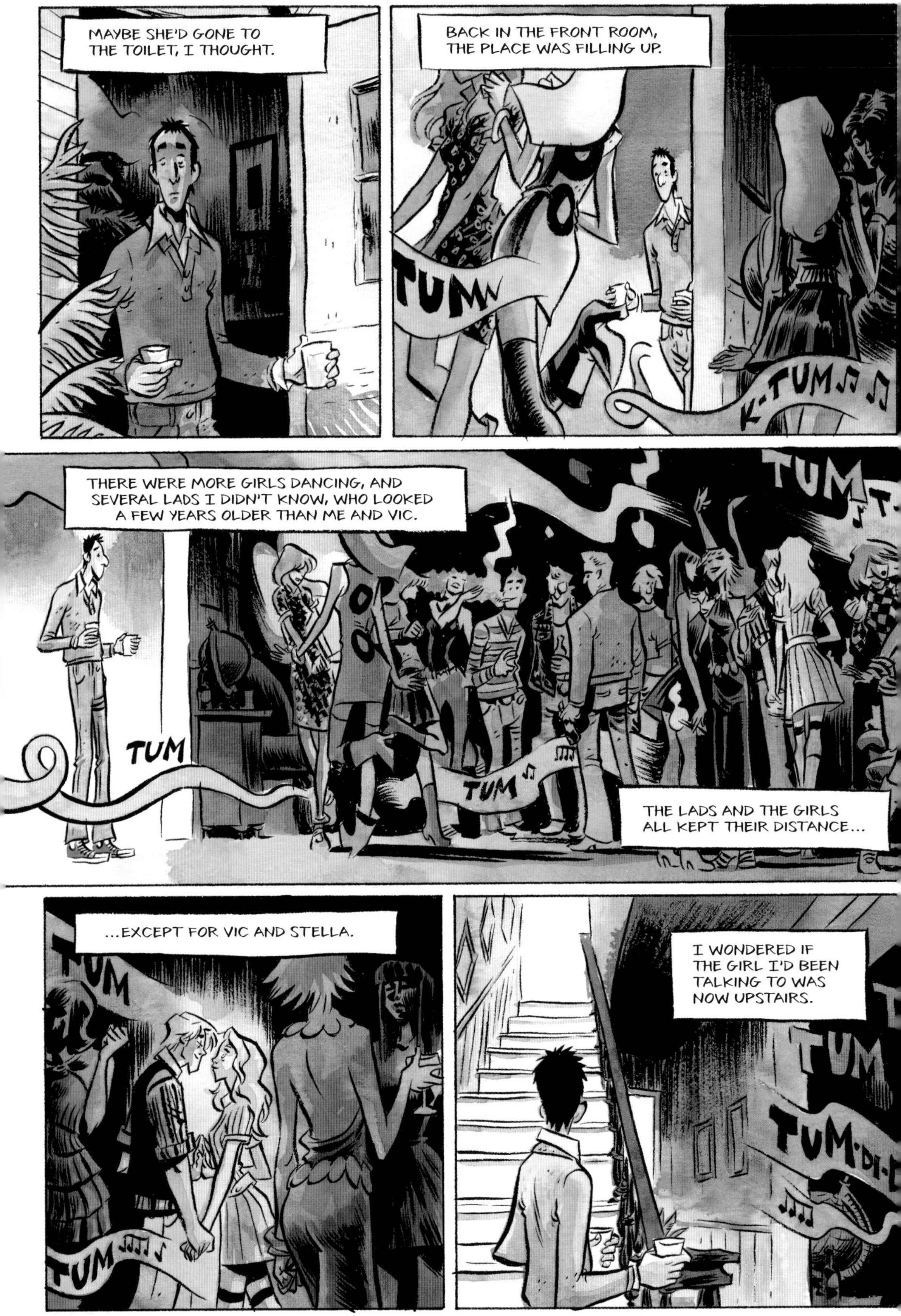
MAYBE SHE'D GONE TO THE TOILET, I THOUGHT.
BACK IN THE FRONT ROOM, THE PLACE WAS FILLING UP.
TUM
K-TUM
THERE WERE MORE GIRLS DANCING, AND SEVERAL LADS I DIDN'T KNOW, WHO LOOKED A FEW YEARS OLDER THAN ME AND VIC.
TUM
TUM
TUM
THE LADS AND THE GIRLS ALL KEPT THEIR DISTANCE...
...EXCEPT FOR VIC AND STELLA.
TUM
TUM
I WONDERED IF THE GIRL I'D BEEN TALKING TO WAS NOW UPSTAIRS.
TUM
TUM-DI-

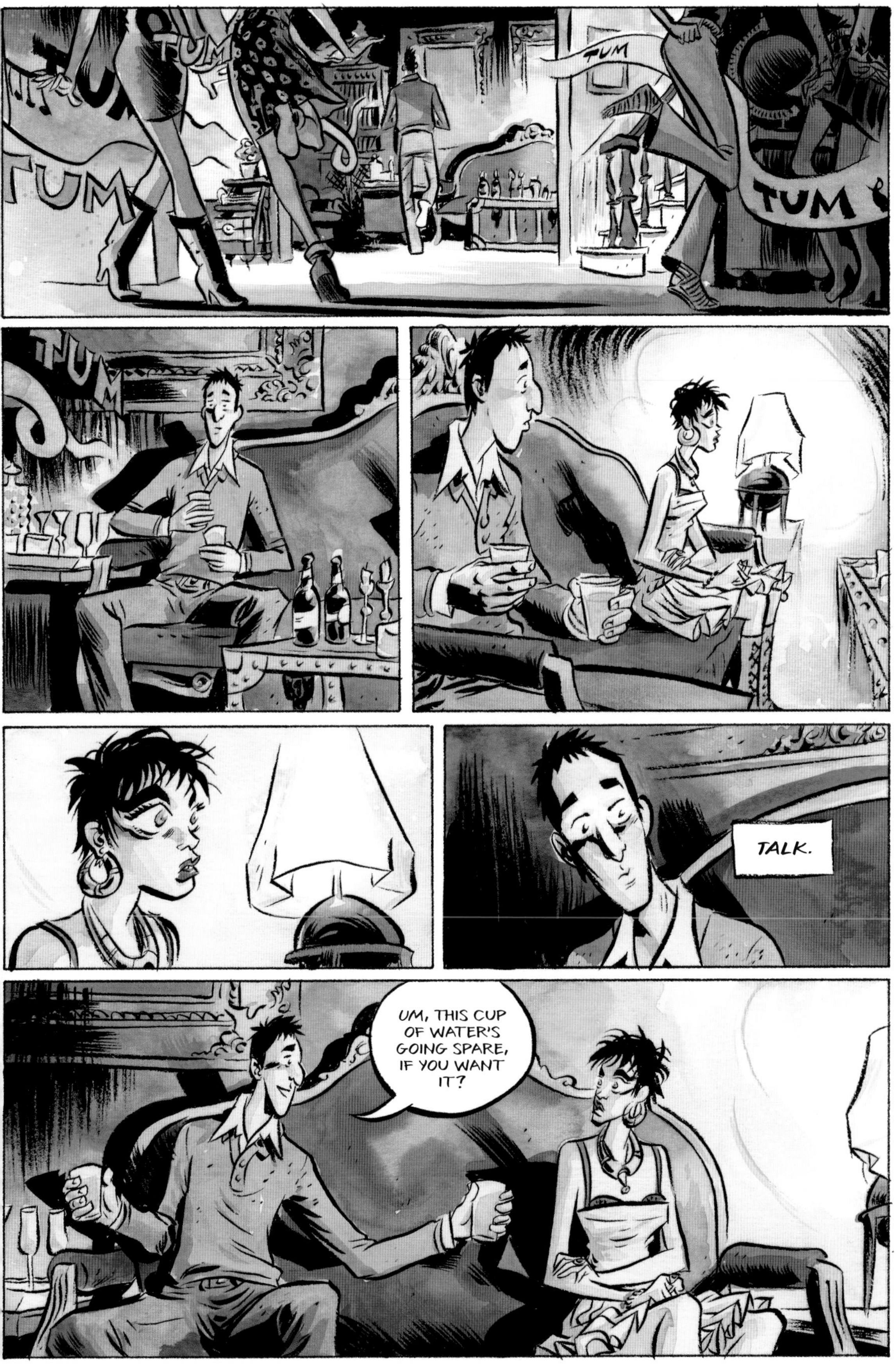
TUM
TUM
TUM
TUM
TUM
TUM
TALK.
UM, THIS CUP OF WATER'S GOING SPARE, IF YOU WANT IT?

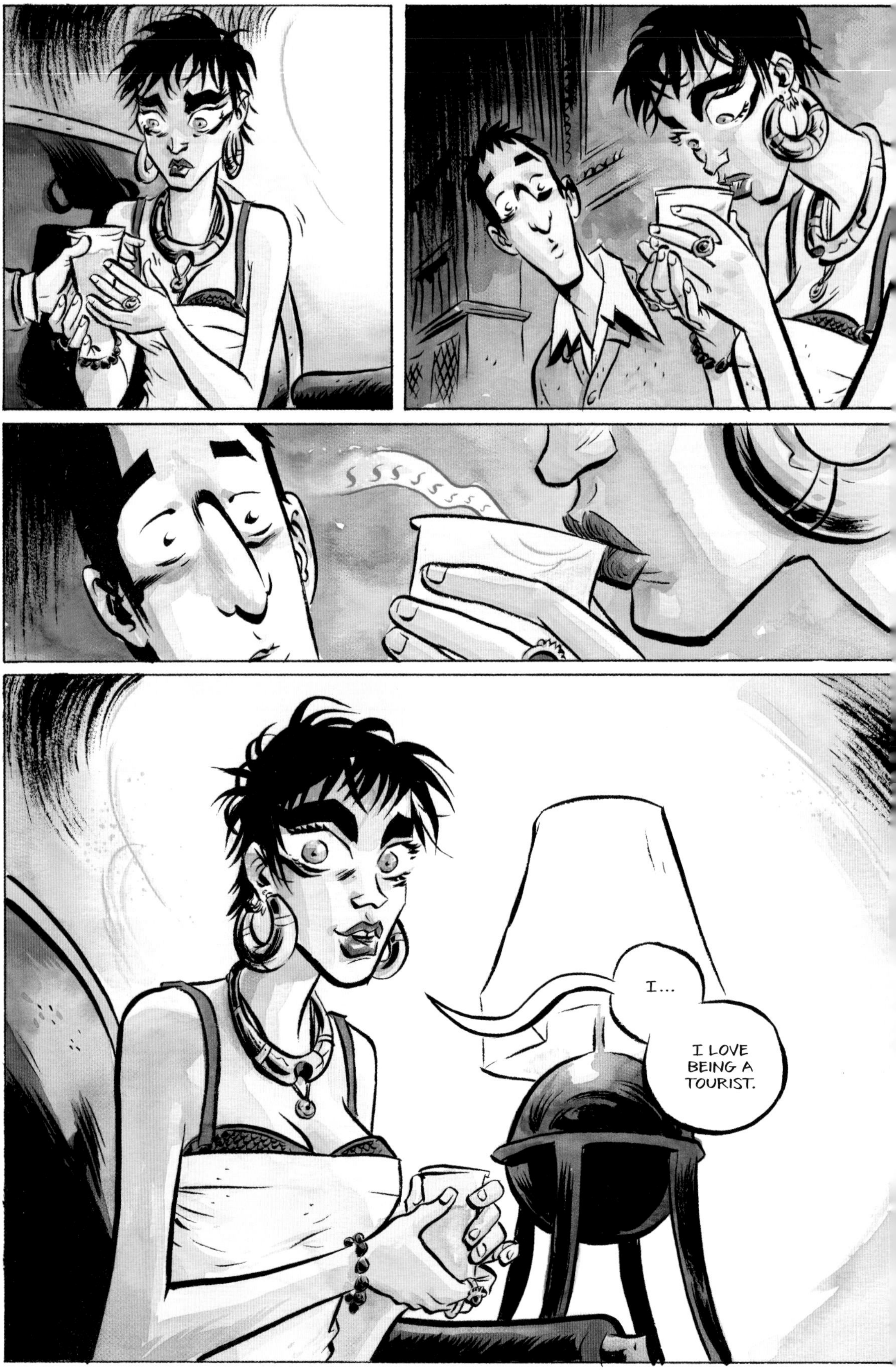
SSSSSSSS
I...
I LOVE BEING A TOURIST.

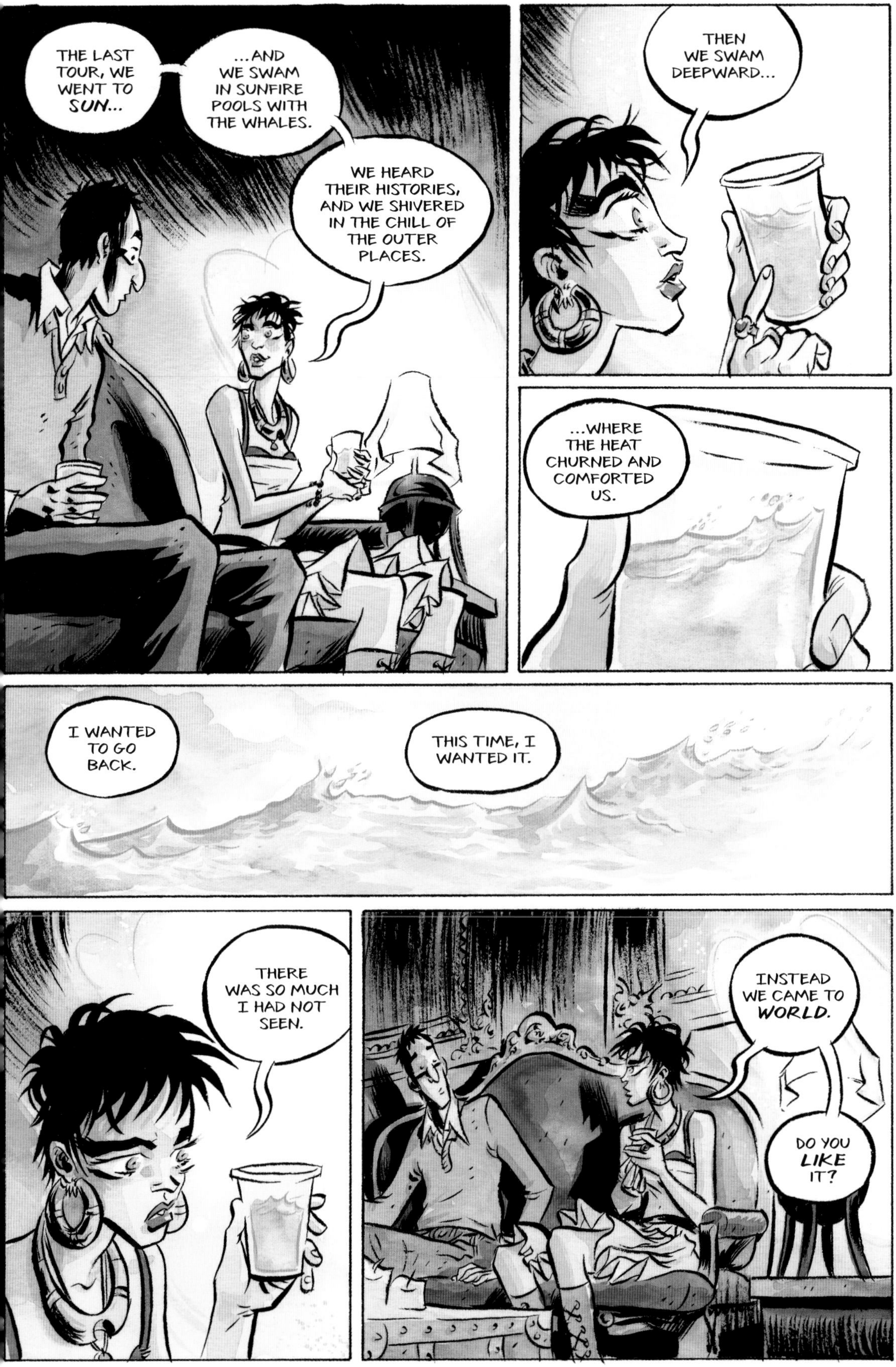
THE LAST TOUR, WE WENT TO SUN...
...AND WE SWAM IN SUNFIRE POOLS WITH THE WHALES.
WE HEARD THEIR HISTORIES, AND WE SHIVERED IN THE CHILL OF THE OUTER PLACES.
THEN WE SWAM DEEPWARD...
...WHERE THE HEAT CHURNED AND COMFORTED US.
I WANTED TO GO BACK.
THIS TIME, I WANTED IT.
THERE WAS SO MUCH I HAD NOT SEEN.
INSTEAD WE CAME TO WORLD.
DO YOU LIKE IT?

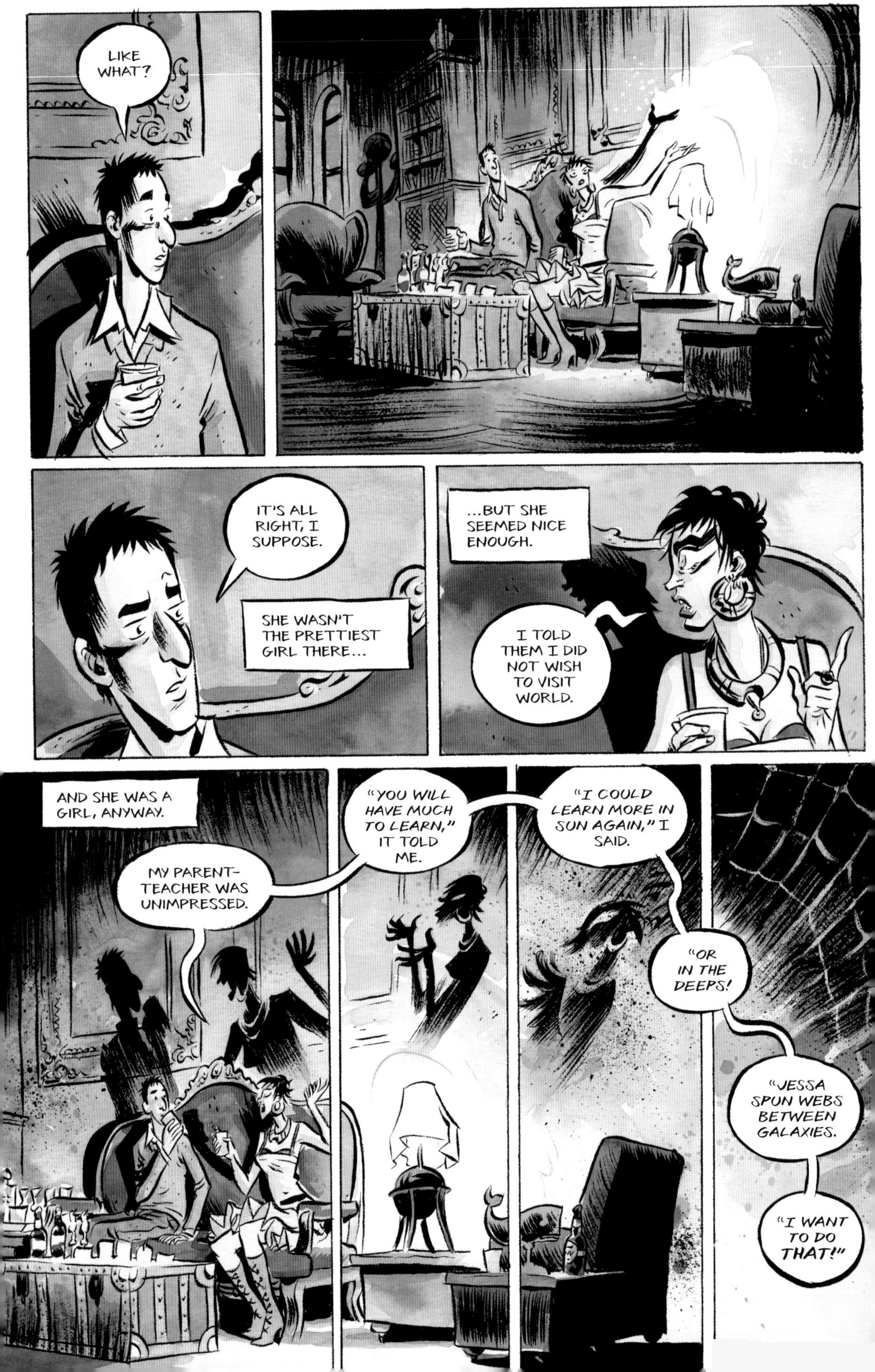
LIKE WHAT?
IT'S ALL RIGHT, I SUPPOSE.
SHE WASN'T THE PRETTIEST GIRL THERE…
…BUT SHE SEEMED NICE ENOUGH.
I TOLD THEM I DID NOT WISH TO VISIT WORLD.
AND SHE WAS A GIRL, ANYWAY.
MY PARENT-TEACHER WAS UNIMPRESSED.
"YOU WILL HAVE MUCH TO LEARN," IT TOLD ME.
"I COULD LEARN MORE IN SUN AGAIN," I SAID.
"OR IN THE DEEPS!
"JESSA SPUN WEBS BETWEEN GALAXIES.
"I WANT TO DO THAT!"

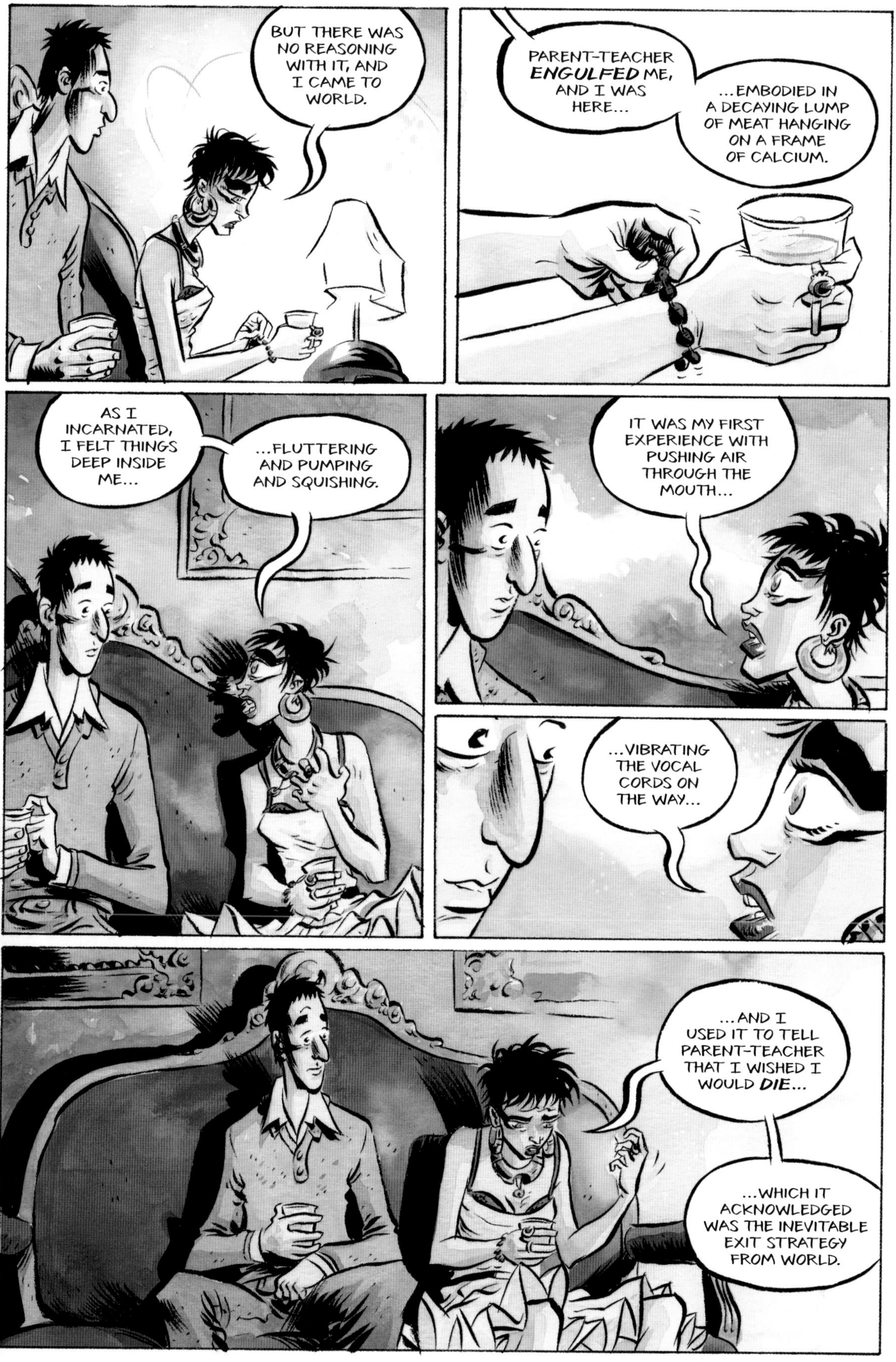
BUT THERE WAS NO REASONING WITH IT, AND I CAME TO WORLD.
PARENT-TEACHER **ENGULFED** ME, AND I WAS HERE...
...EMBODIED IN A DECAYING LUMP OF MEAT HANGING ON A FRAME OF CALCIUM.
AS I INCARNATED, I FELT THINGS DEEP INSIDE ME...
...FLUTTERING AND PUMPING AND SQUISHING.
IT WAS MY FIRST EXPERIENCE WITH PUSHING AIR THROUGH THE MOUTH...
...VIBRATING THE VOCAL CORDS ON THE WAY...
...AND I USED IT TO TELL PARENT-TEACHER THAT I WISHED I WOULD **DIE**...
...WHICH IT ACKNOWLEDGED WAS THE INEVITABLE EXIT STRATEGY FROM WORLD.

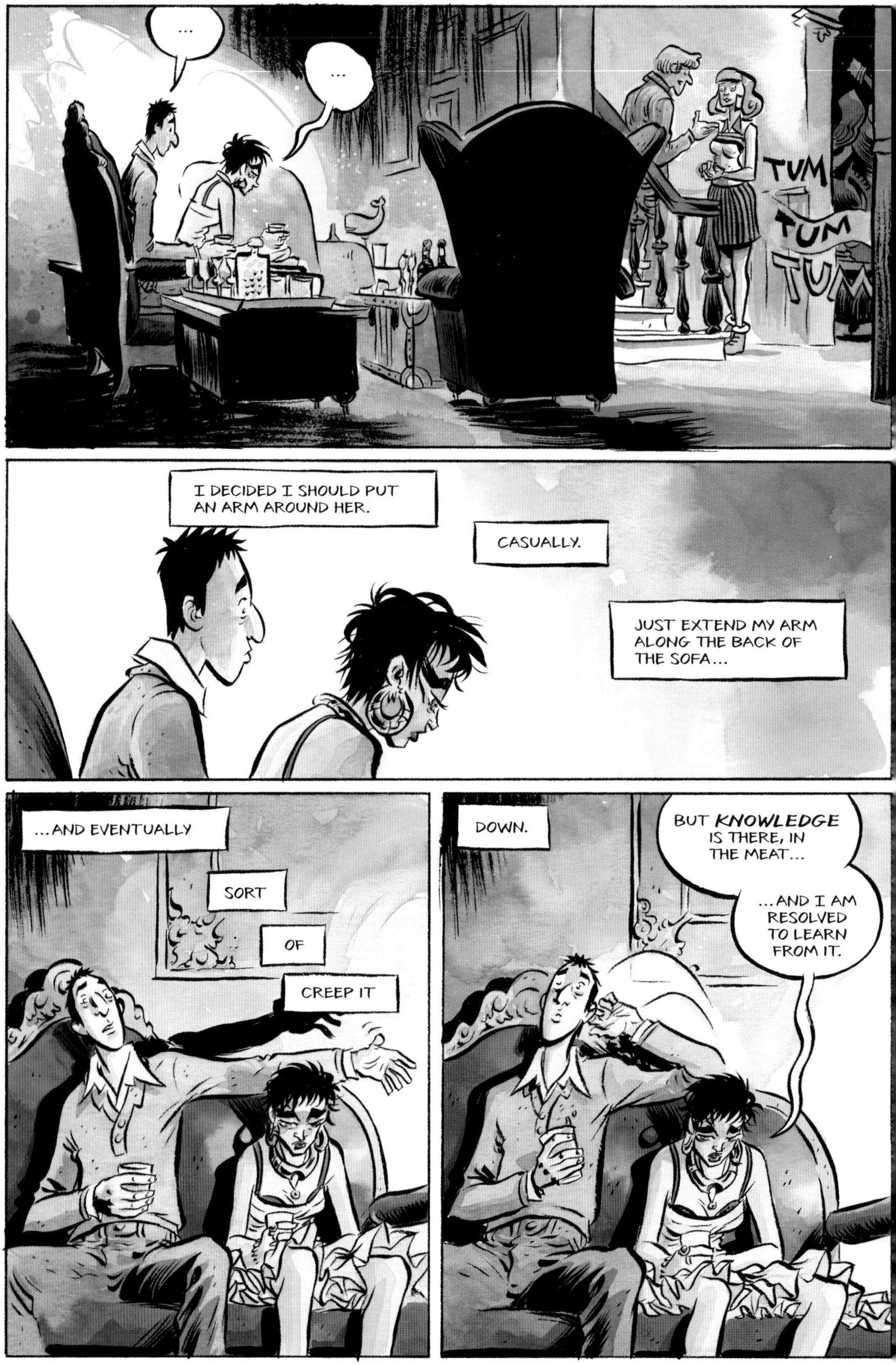
...
...
TUM
TUM
TUM
I DECIDED I SHOULD PUT AN ARM AROUND HER.
CASUALLY.
JUST EXTEND MY ARM ALONG THE BACK OF THE SOFA...
...AND EVENTUALLY
SORT
OF
CREEP IT
DOWN.
BUT **KNOWLEDGE** IS THERE, IN THE MEAT...
...AND I AM RESOLVED TO LEARN FROM IT.

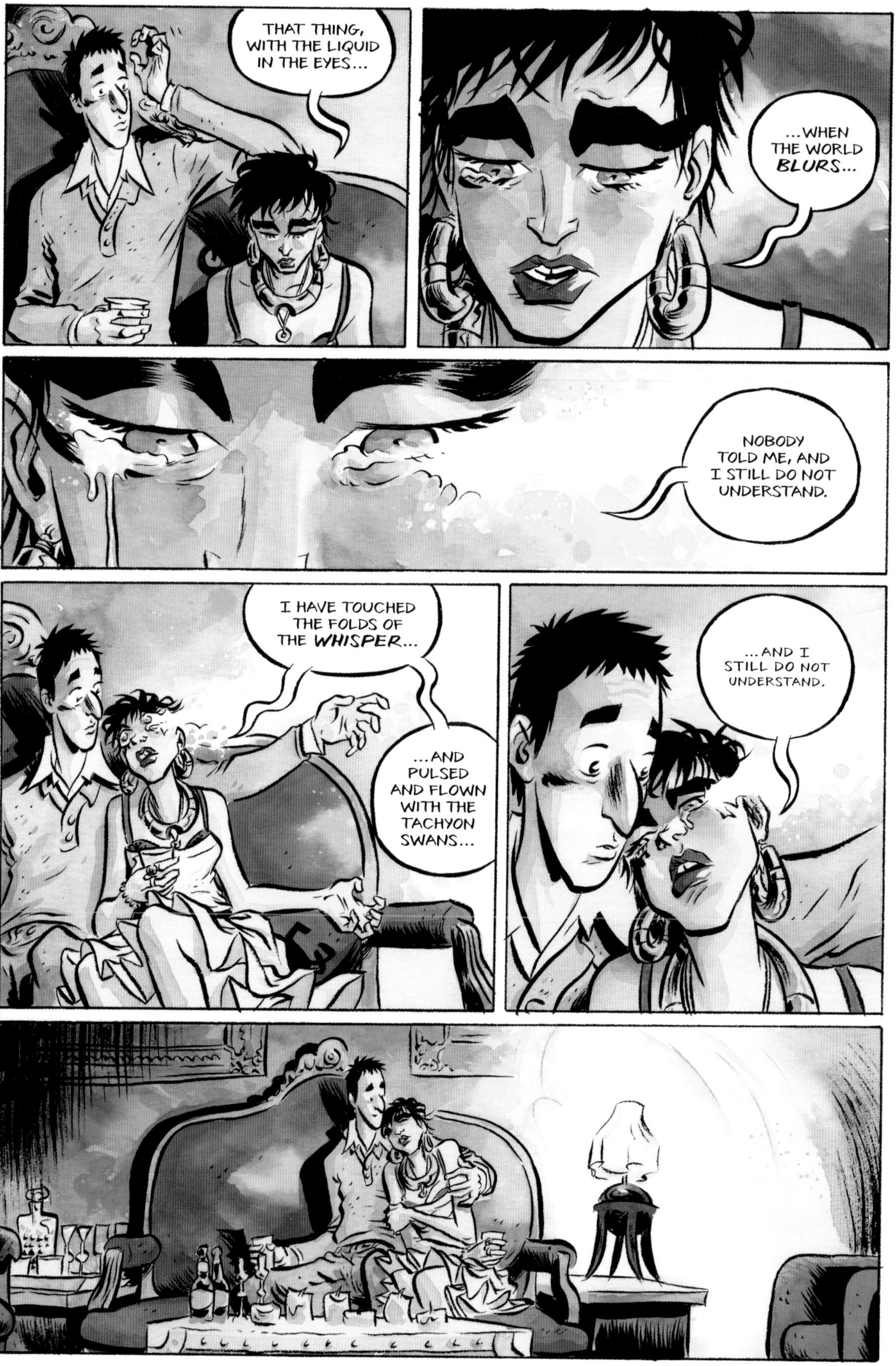
THAT THING, WITH THE LIQUID IN THE EYES...
...WHEN THE WORLD BLURS...
NOBODY TOLD ME, AND I STILL DO NOT UNDERSTAND.
I HAVE TOUCHED THE FOLDS OF THE WHISPER...
...AND PULSED AND FLOWN WITH THE TACHYON SWANS...
...AND I STILL DO NOT UNDERSTAND.

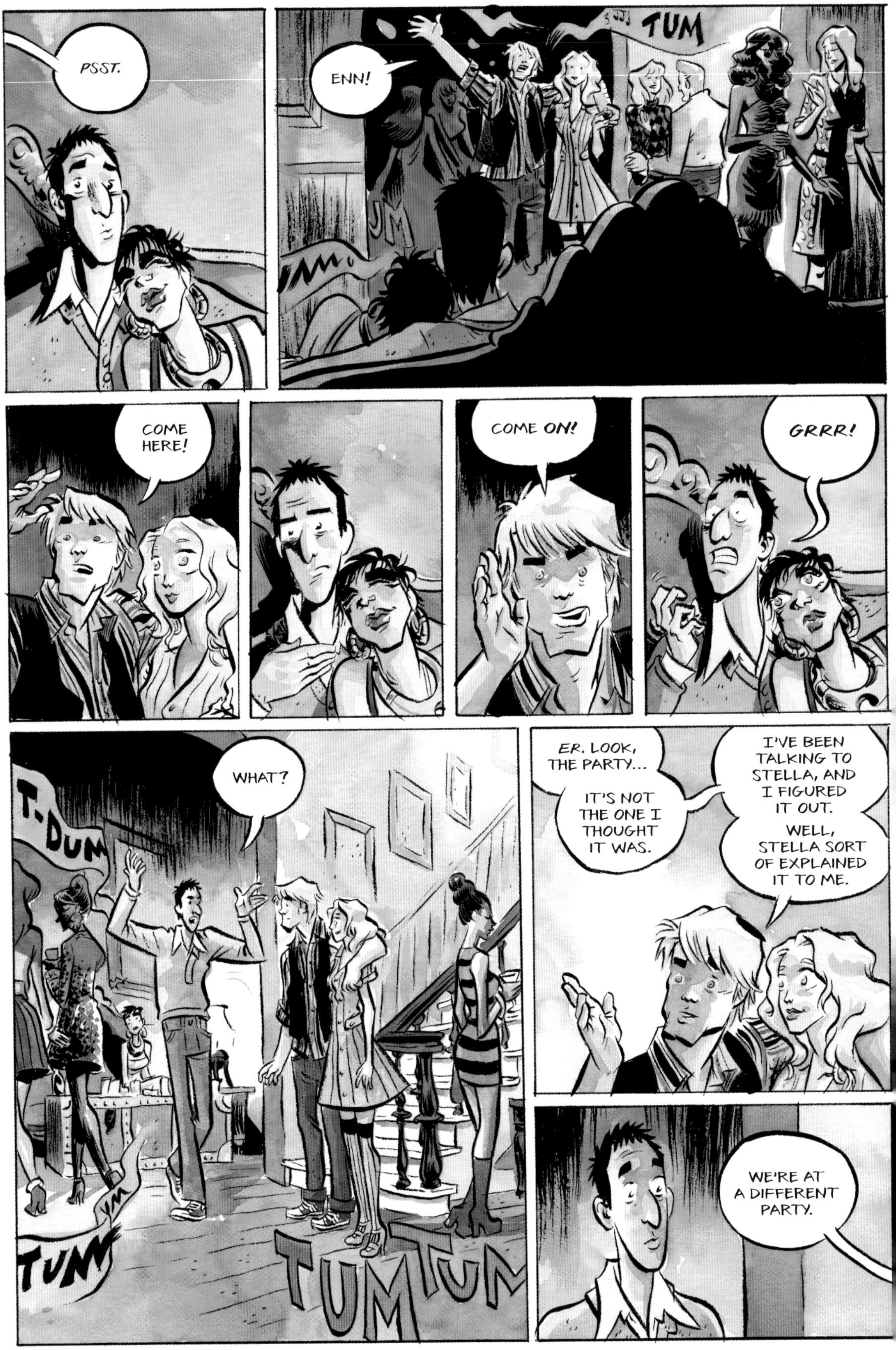
PSST.
ENN!
TUM
COME HERE!
COME ON!
GRRR!
T-DUM
WHAT?
TUM TUM
ER. LOOK, THE PARTY...
IT'S NOT THE ONE I THOUGHT IT WAS.
I'VE BEEN TALKING TO STELLA, AND I FIGURED IT OUT.
WELL, STELLA SORT OF EXPLAINED IT TO ME.
WE'RE AT A DIFFERENT PARTY.

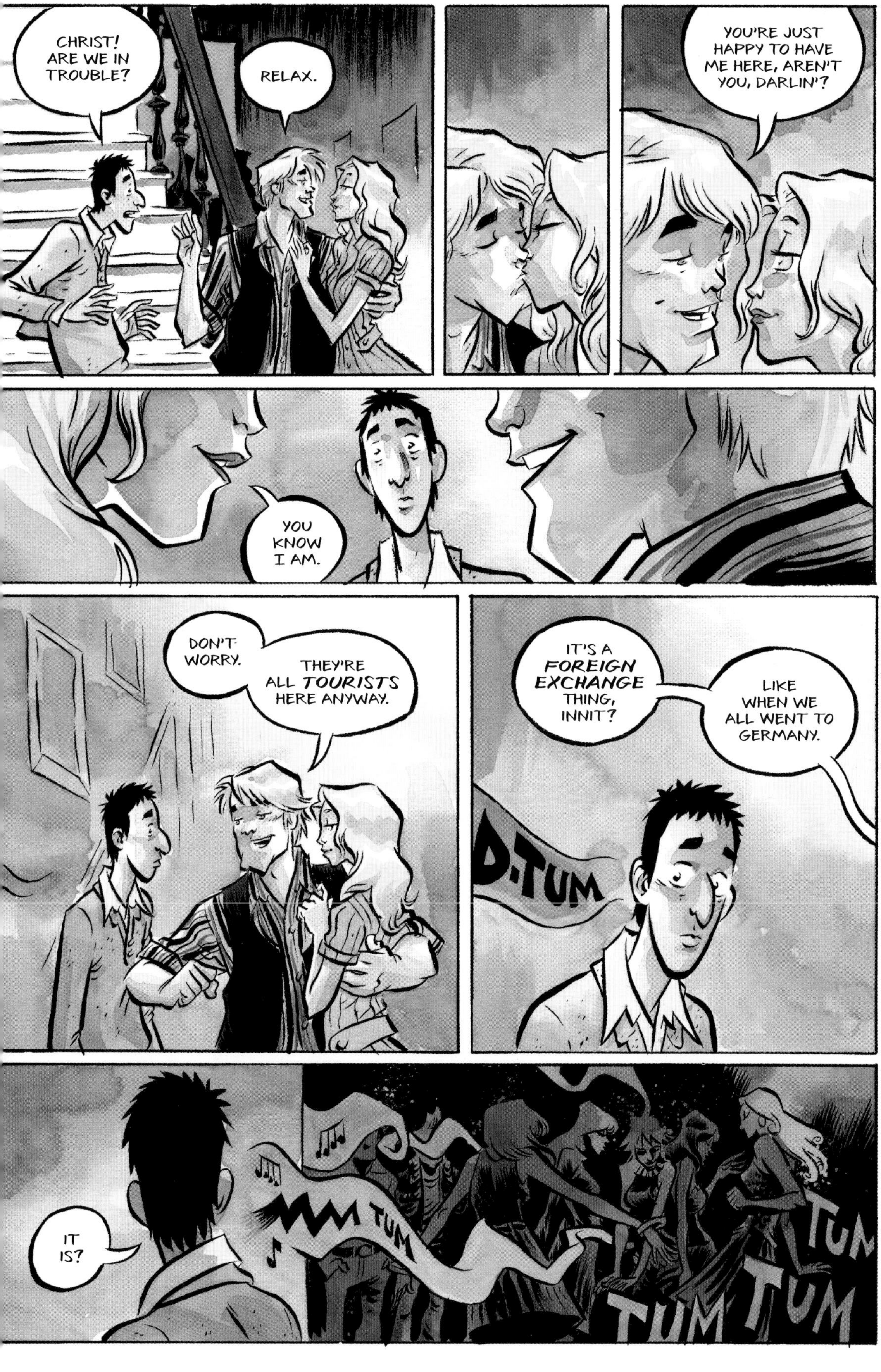
CHRIST! ARE WE IN TROUBLE?
RELAX.
YOU'RE JUST HAPPY TO HAVE ME HERE, AREN'T YOU, DARLIN'?
YOU KNOW I AM.
DON'T WORRY.
THEY'RE ALL TOURISTS HERE ANYWAY.
IT'S A FOREIGN EXCHANGE THING, INNIT?
LIKE WHEN WE ALL WENT TO GERMANY.
D.TUM
IT IS?
TUM
TUM
TUM TUM

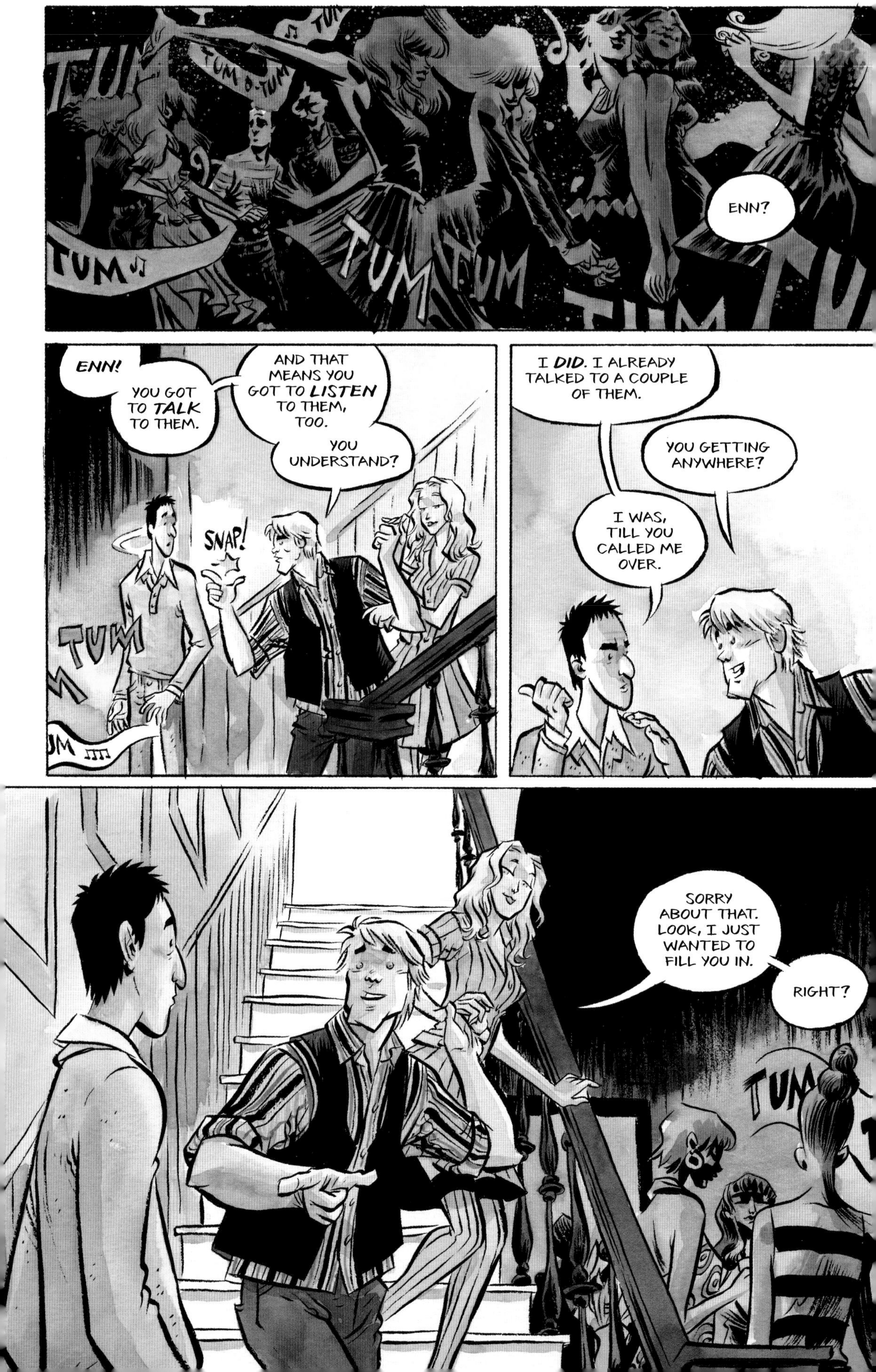
TUM
TUM
TUM-D-TUM
TUM
TUM TUM
TUM
TUM
ENN?
ENN!
YOU GOT TO TALK TO THEM.
AND THAT MEANS YOU GOT TO LISTEN TO THEM, TOO.
YOU UNDERSTAND?
SNAP!
TUM
UM
I DID. I ALREADY TALKED TO A COUPLE OF THEM.
YOU GETTING ANYWHERE?
I WAS, TILL YOU CALLED ME OVER.
SORRY ABOUT THAT. LOOK, I JUST WANTED TO FILL YOU IN.
RIGHT?
TUM

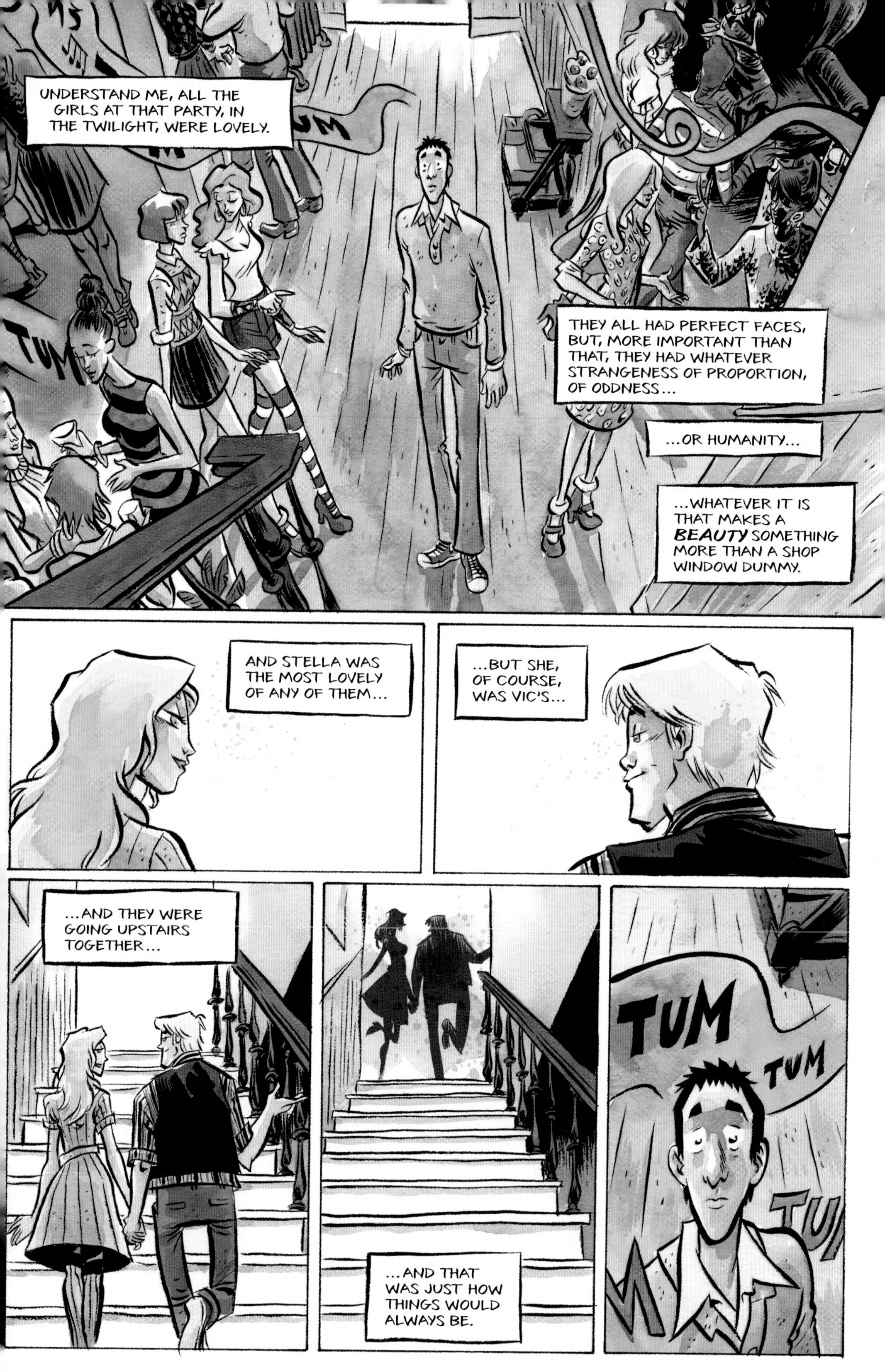
UNDERSTAND ME, ALL THE GIRLS AT THAT PARTY, IN THE TWILIGHT, WERE LOVELY.
TUM
THEY ALL HAD PERFECT FACES, BUT, MORE IMPORTANT THAN THAT, THEY HAD WHATEVER STRANGENESS OF PROPORTION, OF ODDNESS…
…OR HUMANITY…
…WHATEVER IT IS THAT MAKES A ***BEAUTY*** SOMETHING MORE THAN A SHOP WINDOW DUMMY.
AND STELLA WAS THE MOST LOVELY OF ANY OF THEM…
…BUT SHE, OF COURSE, WAS VIC'S…
…AND THEY WERE GOING UPSTAIRS TOGETHER…
…AND THAT WAS JUST HOW THINGS WOULD ALWAYS BE.
TUM
TUM

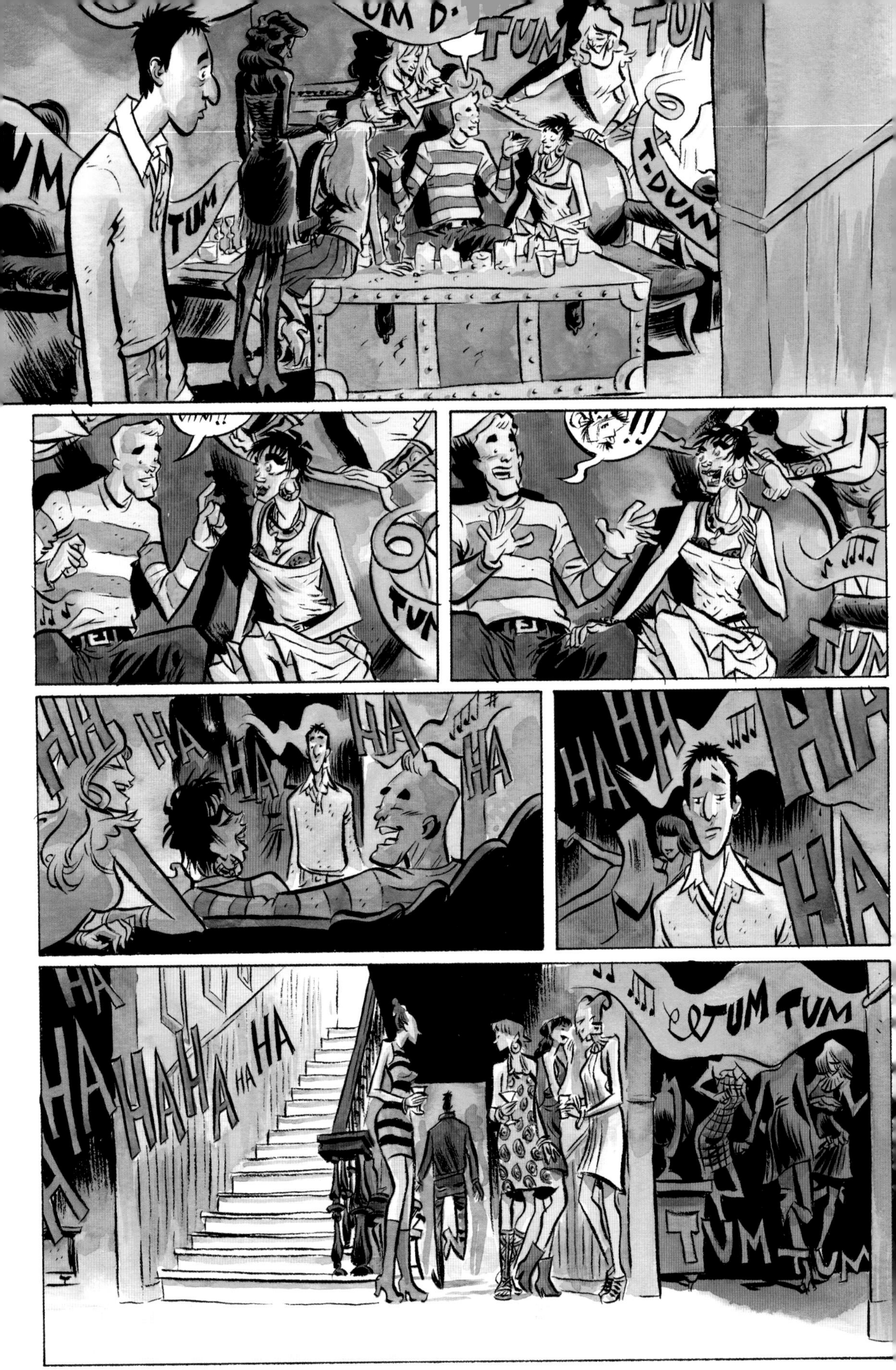

TUM
TUM
T-DUM
TUM
TUM
TUM
HA HA HA HA HA HA
HA HA HA HA HA
HA HA HA HA ha HA
TUM TUM
TUM TUM

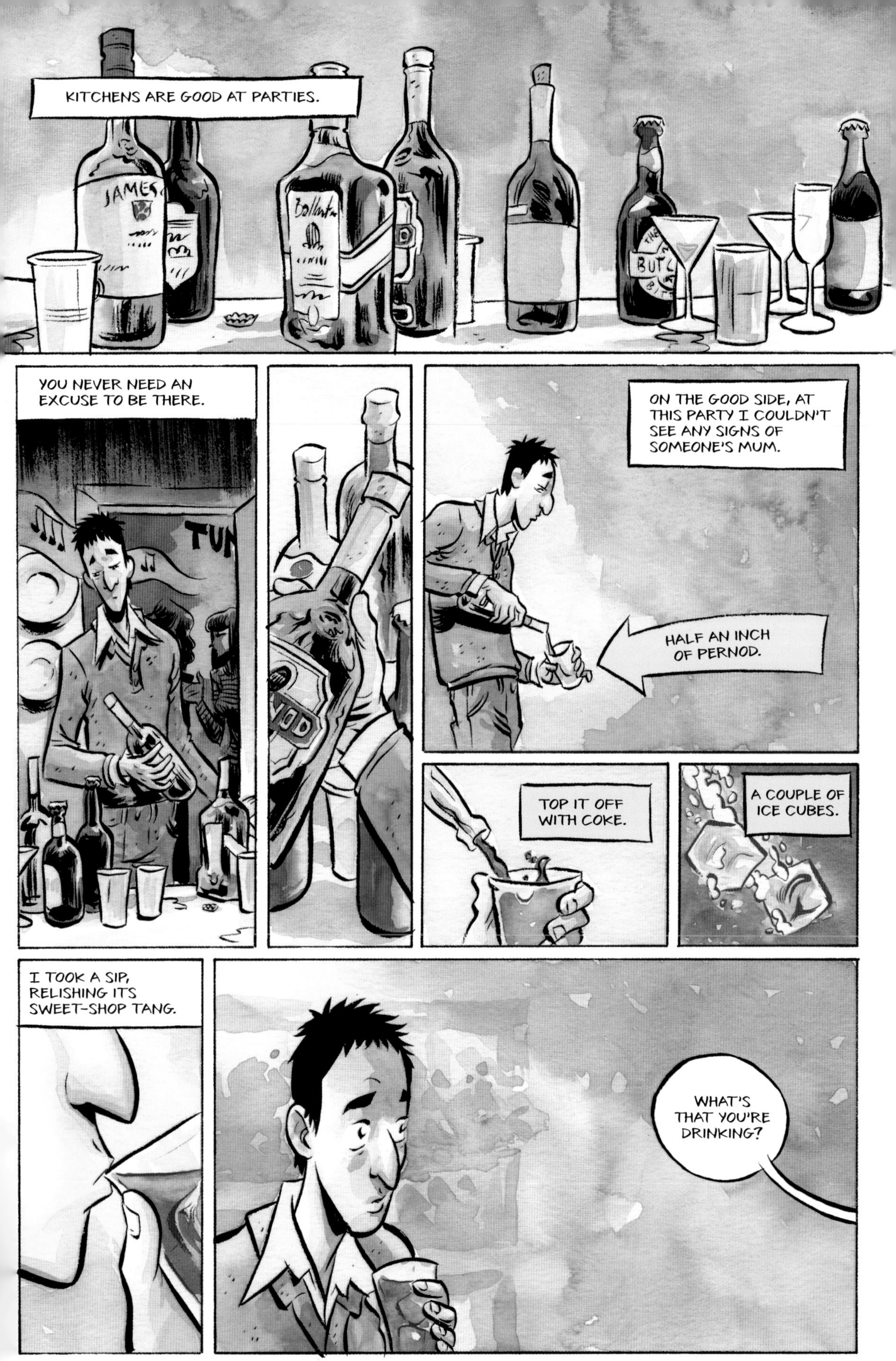

KITCHENS ARE GOOD AT PARTIES.
YOU NEVER NEED AN EXCUSE TO BE THERE.
ON THE GOOD SIDE, AT THIS PARTY I COULDN'T SEE ANY SIGNS OF SOMEONE'S MUM.
HALF AN INCH OF PERNOD.
TOP IT OFF WITH COKE.
A COUPLE OF ICE CUBES.
I TOOK A SIP, RELISHING ITS SWEET-SHOP TANG.
WHAT'S THAT YOU'RE DRINKING?

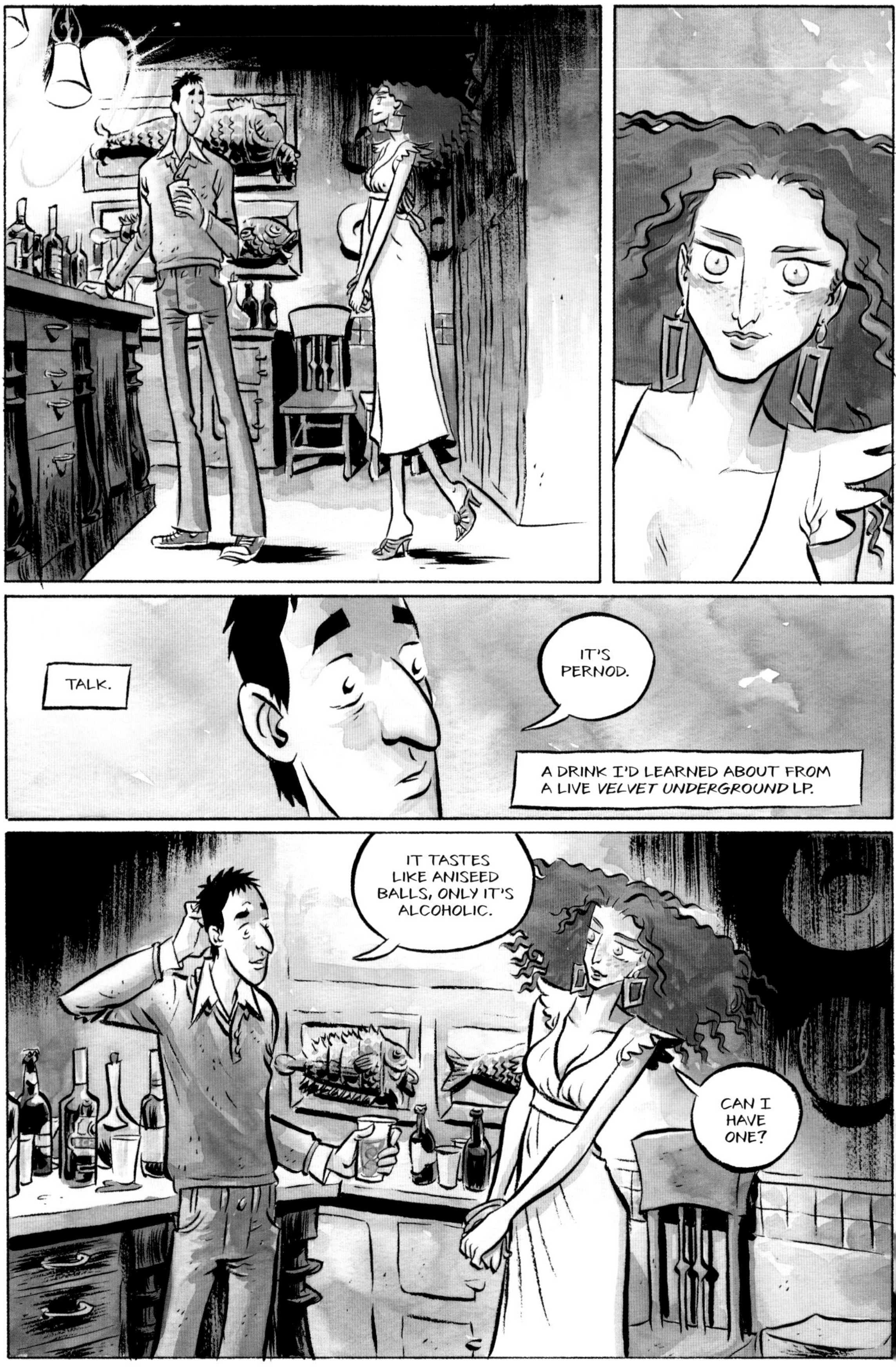
TALK.
IT'S PERNOD.
A DRINK I'D LEARNED ABOUT FROM A LIVE *VELVET UNDERGROUND* LP.
IT TASTES LIKE ANISEED BALLS, ONLY IT'S ALCOHOLIC.
CAN I HAVE ONE?

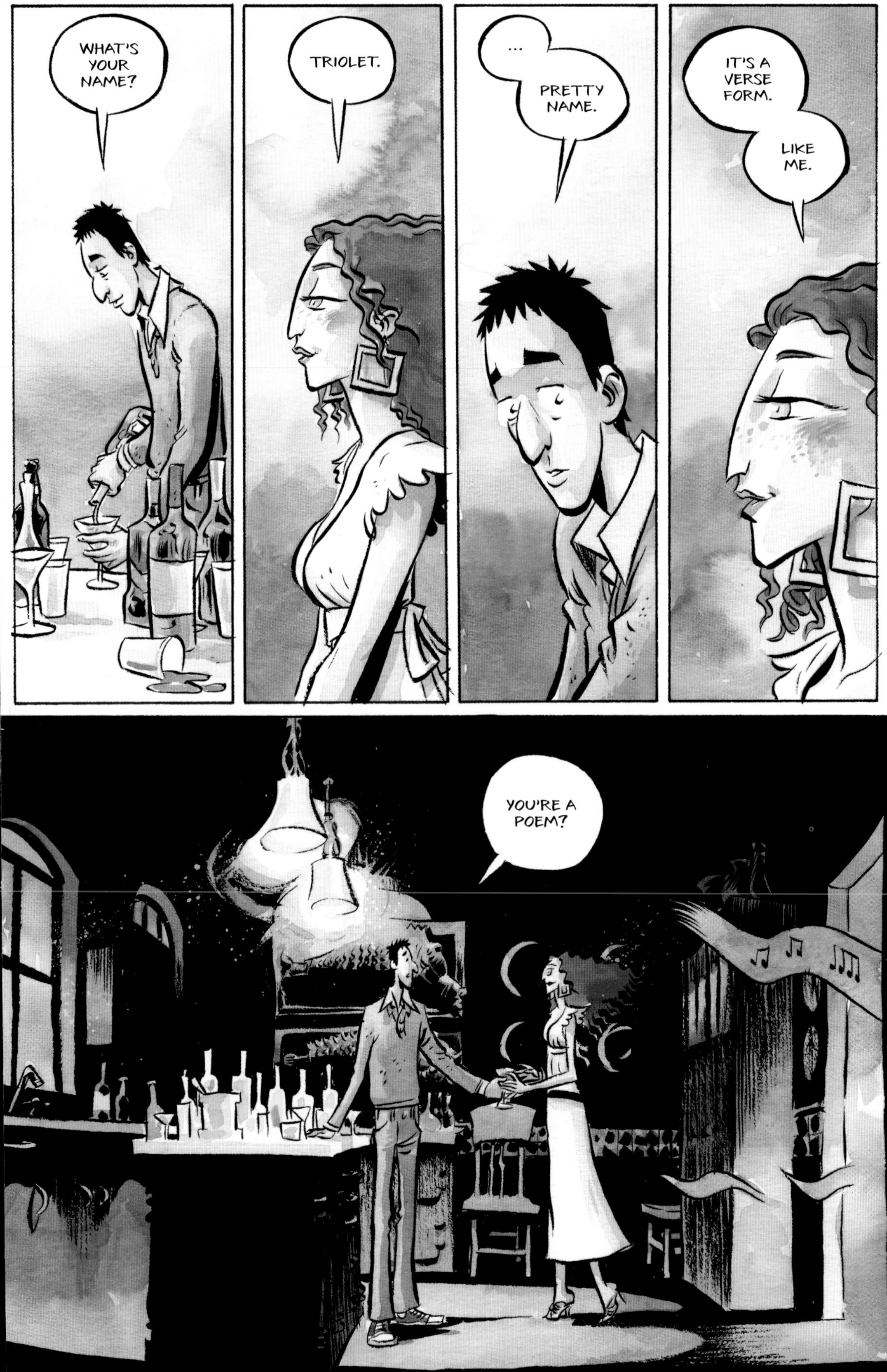
WHAT'S YOUR NAME?
TRIOLET.
...
PRETTY NAME.
IT'S A VERSE FORM.
LIKE ME.
YOU'RE A POEM?

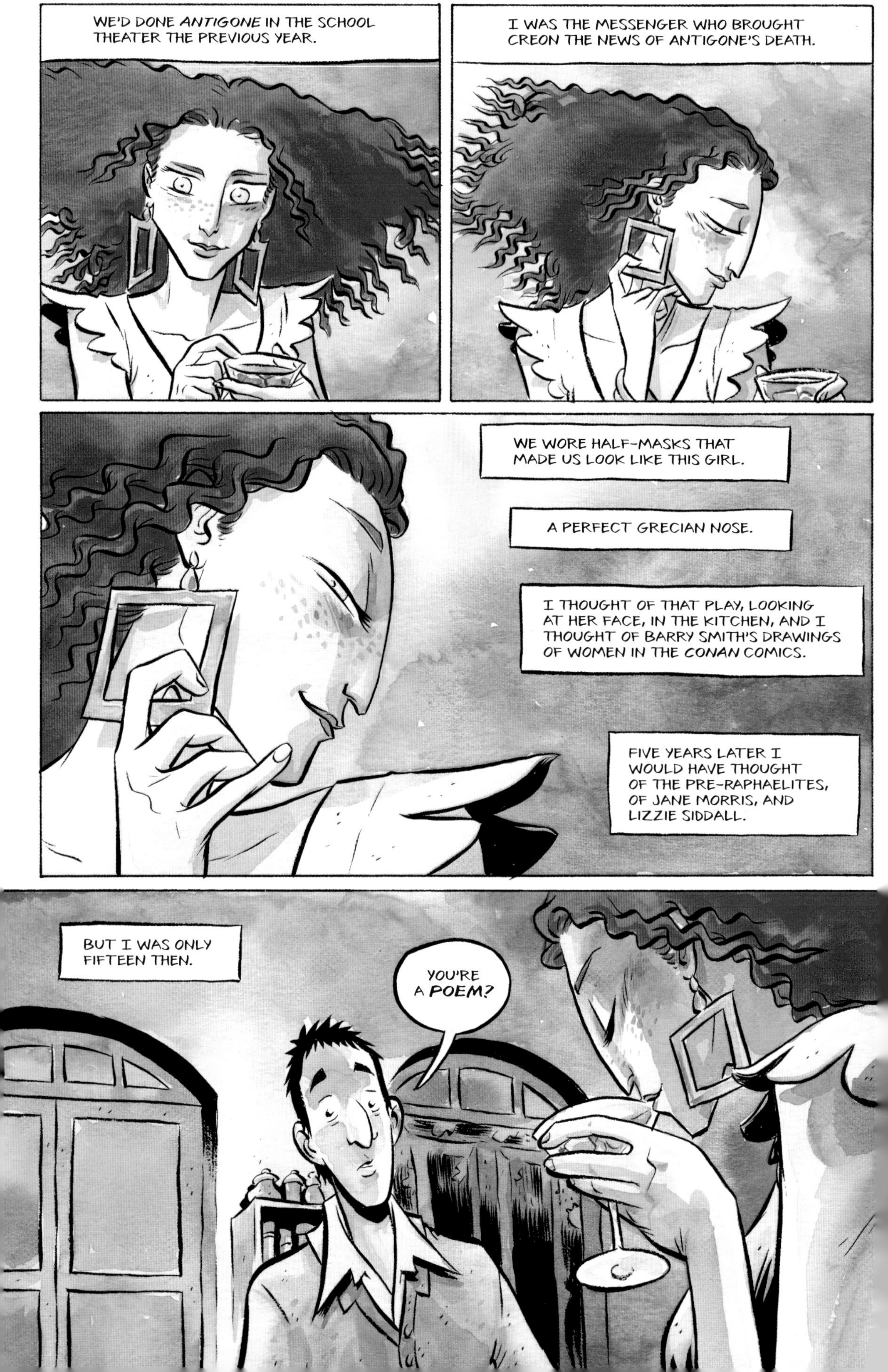
WE'D DONE *ANTIGONE* IN THE SCHOOL THEATER THE PREVIOUS YEAR.
I WAS THE MESSENGER WHO BROUGHT CREON THE NEWS OF ANTIGONE'S DEATH.
WE WORE HALF-MASKS THAT MADE US LOOK LIKE THIS GIRL.
A PERFECT GRECIAN NOSE.
I THOUGHT OF THAT PLAY, LOOKING AT HER FACE, IN THE KITCHEN, AND I THOUGHT OF BARRY SMITH'S DRAWINGS OF WOMEN IN THE *CONAN* COMICS.
FIVE YEARS LATER I WOULD HAVE THOUGHT OF THE PRE-RAPHAELITES, OF JANE MORRIS, AND LIZZIE SIDDALL.
BUT I WAS ONLY FIFTEEN THEN.
YOU'RE A ***POEM?***

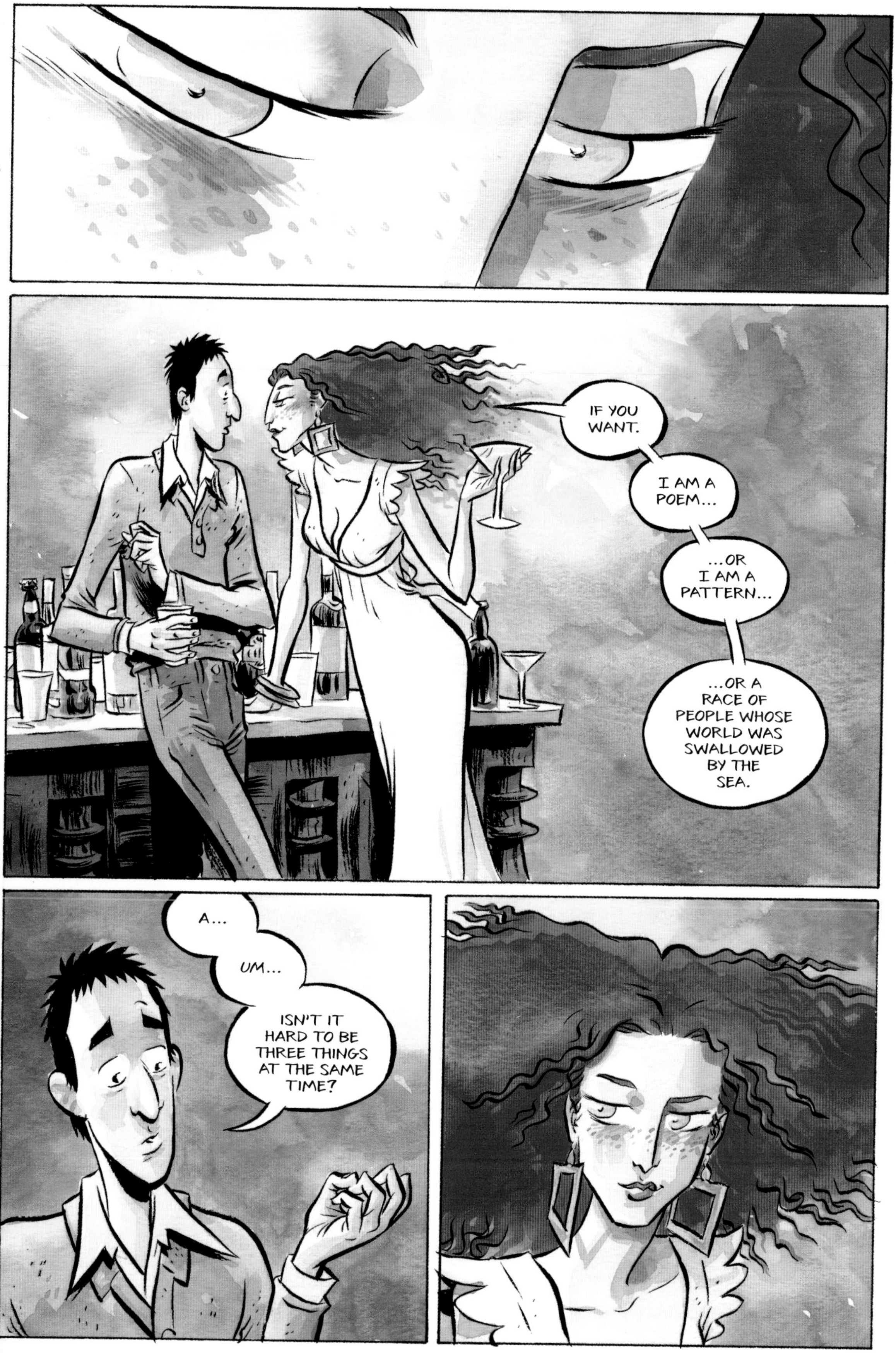
IF YOU WANT.
I AM A POEM...
...OR I AM A PATTERN...
...OR A RACE OF PEOPLE WHOSE WORLD WAS SWALLOWED BY THE SEA.
A...
UM...
ISN'T IT HARD TO BE THREE THINGS AT THE SAME TIME?

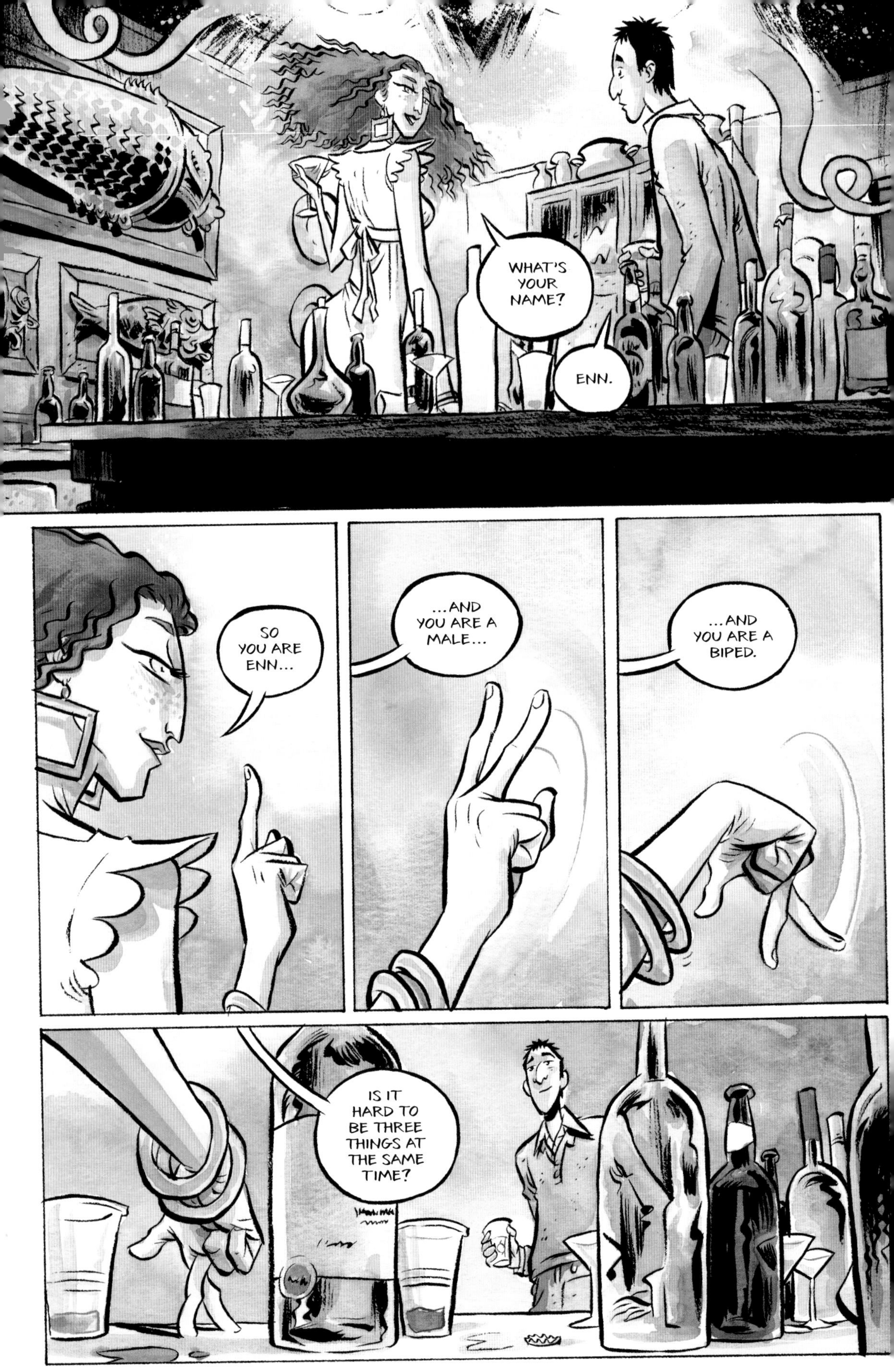
WHAT'S YOUR NAME?
ENN.
SO YOU ARE ENN...
...AND YOU ARE A MALE...
...AND YOU ARE A BIPED.
IS IT HARD TO BE THREE THINGS AT THE SAME TIME?

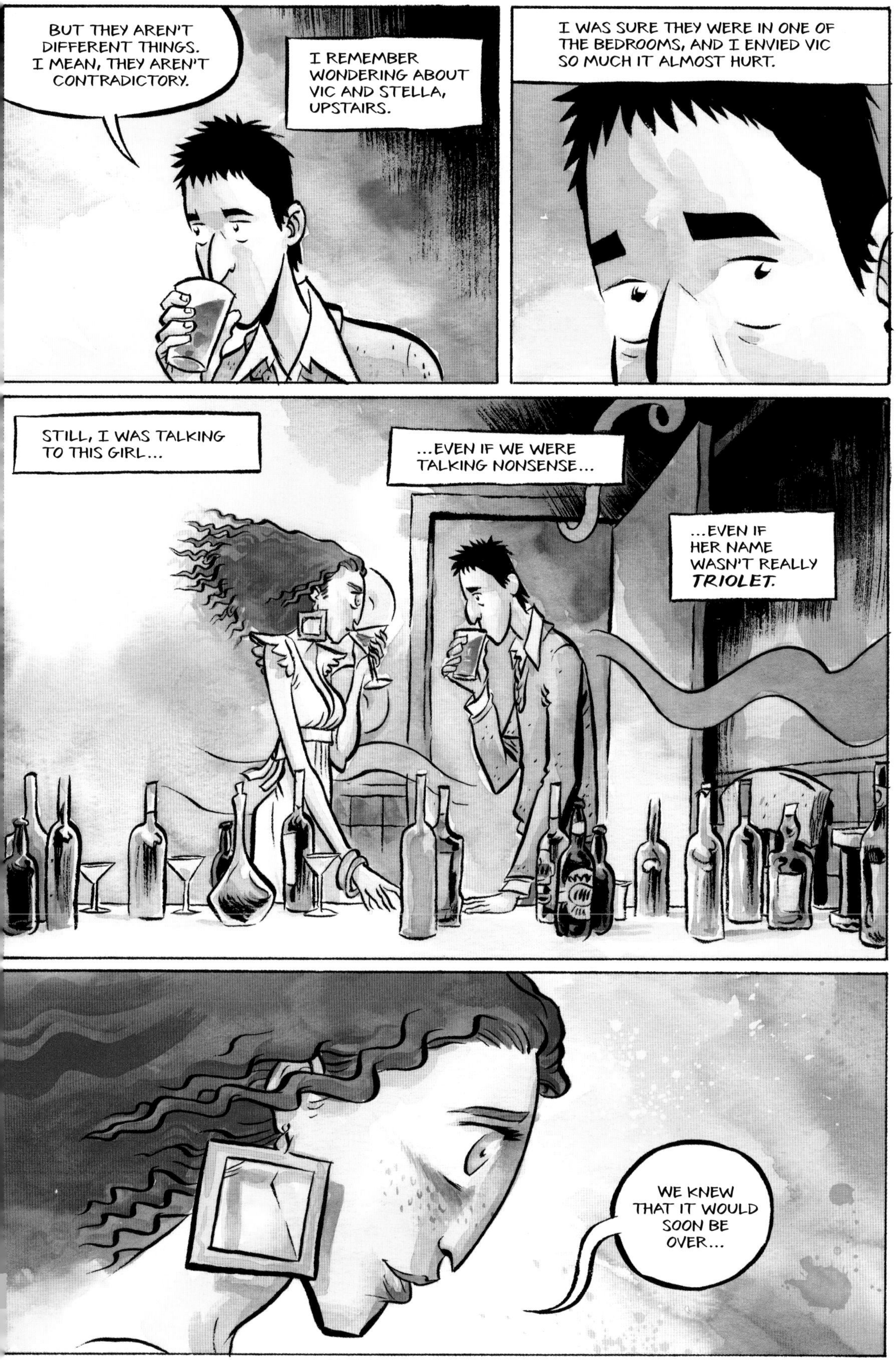
BUT THEY AREN'T DIFFERENT THINGS. I MEAN, THEY AREN'T CONTRADICTORY.
I REMEMBER WONDERING ABOUT VIC AND STELLA, UPSTAIRS.
I WAS SURE THEY WERE IN ONE OF THE BEDROOMS, AND I ENVIED VIC SO MUCH IT ALMOST HURT.
STILL, I WAS TALKING TO THIS GIRL...
...EVEN IF WE WERE TALKING NONSENSE...
...EVEN IF HER NAME WASN'T REALLY *TRIOLET*.
WE KNEW THAT IT WOULD SOON BE OVER...

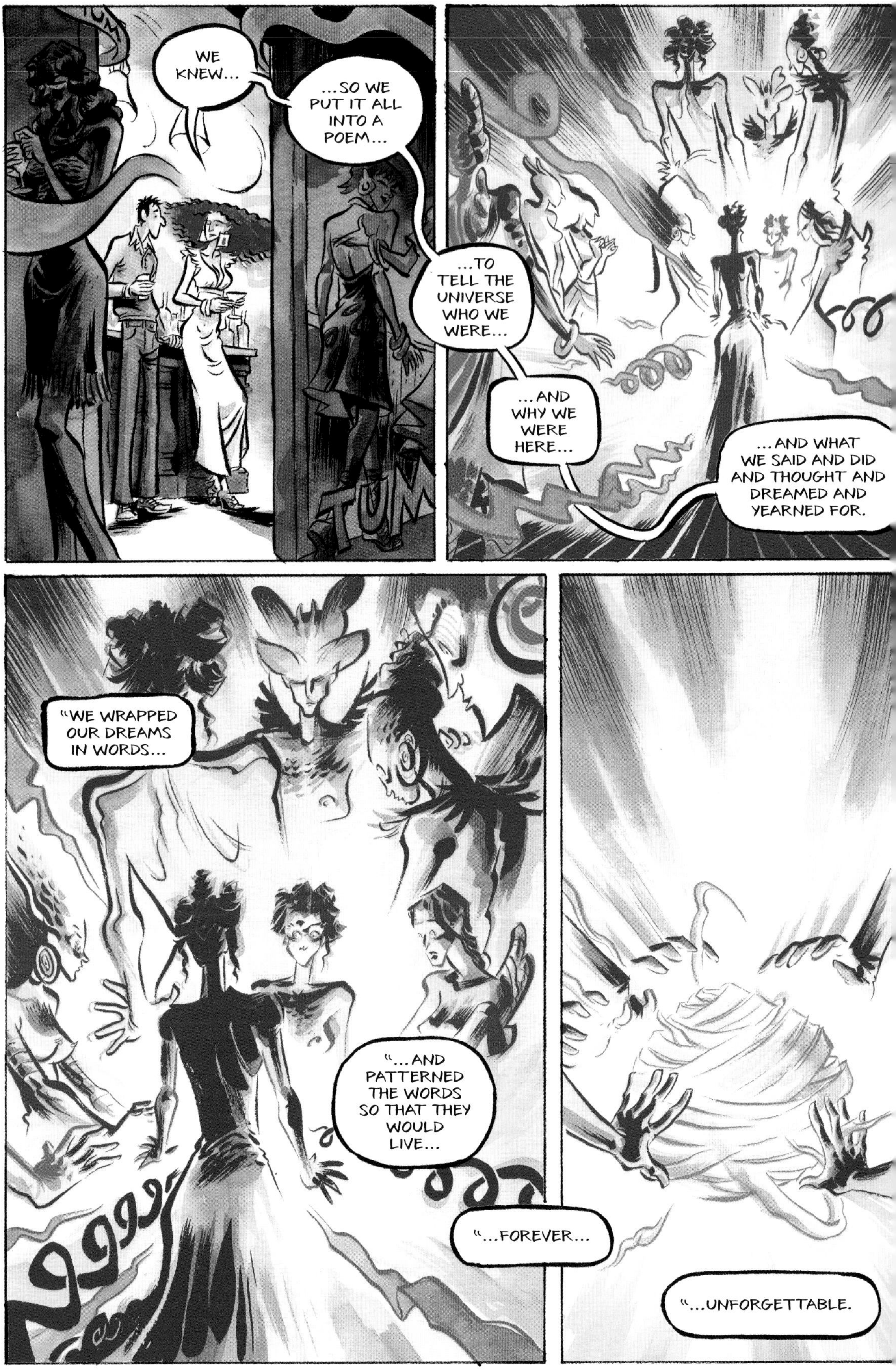
WE KNEW...
...SO WE PUT IT ALL INTO A POEM...
...TO TELL THE UNIVERSE WHO WE WERE...
...AND WHY WE WERE HERE...
...AND WHAT WE SAID AND DID AND THOUGHT AND DREAMED AND YEARNED FOR.
TUM
"WE WRAPPED OUR DREAMS IN WORDS...
"...AND PATTERNED THE WORDS SO THAT THEY WOULD LIVE...
"...FOREVER...
"...UNFORGETTABLE.

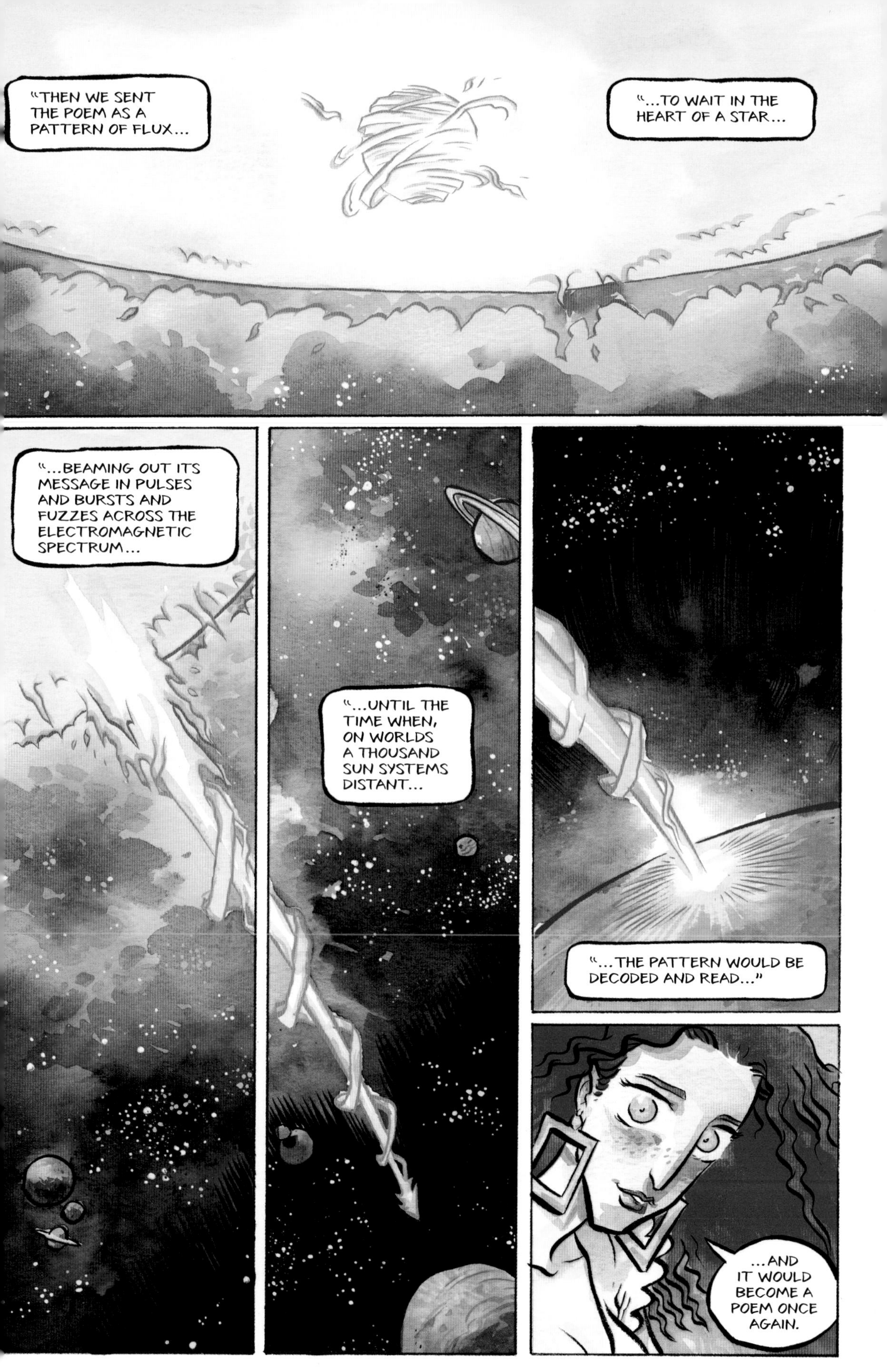
"THEN WE SENT THE POEM AS A PATTERN OF FLUX...
"...TO WAIT IN THE HEART OF A STAR...
"...BEAMING OUT ITS MESSAGE IN PULSES AND BURSTS AND FUZZES ACROSS THE ELECTROMAGNETIC SPECTRUM...
"...UNTIL THE TIME WHEN, ON WORLDS A THOUSAND SUN SYSTEMS DISTANT...
"...THE PATTERN WOULD BE DECODED AND READ..."
...AND IT WOULD BECOME A POEM ONCE AGAIN.

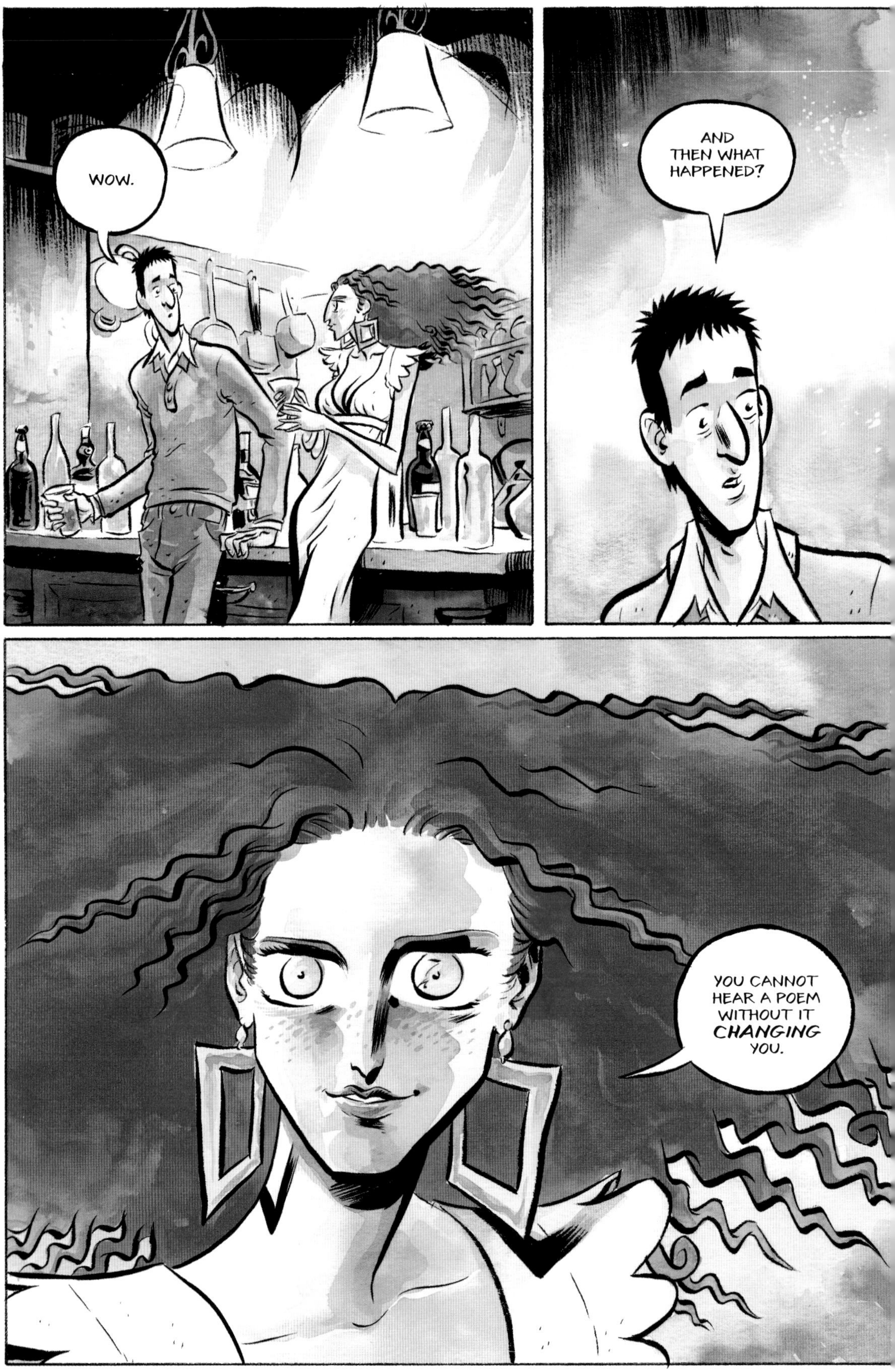
WOW.
AND THEN WHAT HAPPENED?
YOU CANNOT HEAR A POEM WITHOUT IT *CHANGING* YOU.

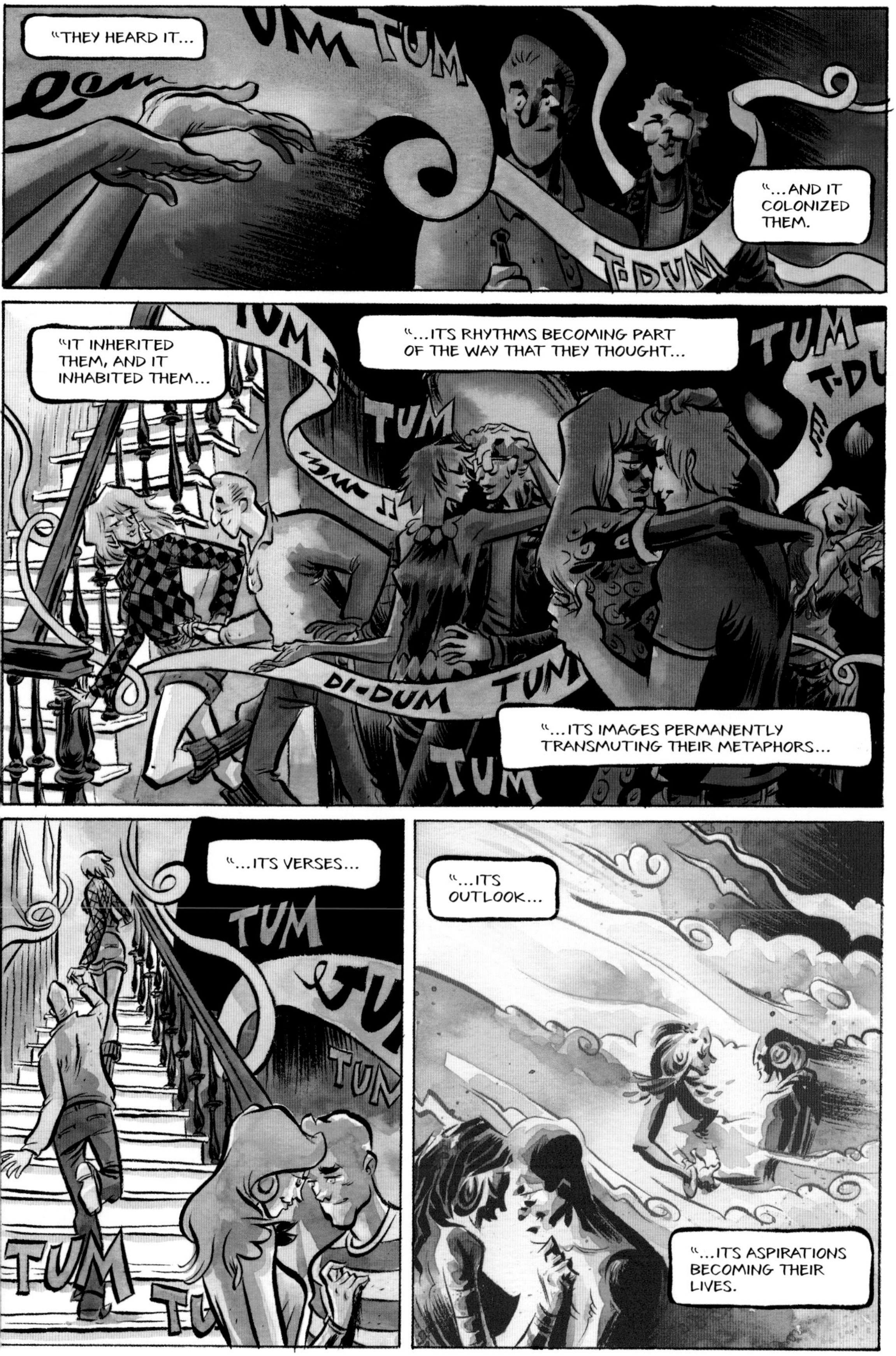
"THEY HEARD IT...
TUM TUM
T-DUM
"...AND IT COLONIZED THEM.
"IT INHERITED THEM, AND IT INHABITED THEM...
"...ITS RHYTHMS BECOMING PART OF THE WAY THAT THEY THOUGHT...
TUM
TUM
T-DU
DI-DUM TUM
"...ITS IMAGES PERMANENTLY TRANSMUTING THEIR METAPHORS...
TUM
"...ITS VERSES...
TUM
TUM
TUM
"...ITS OUTLOOK...
"...ITS ASPIRATIONS BECOMING THEIR LIVES.

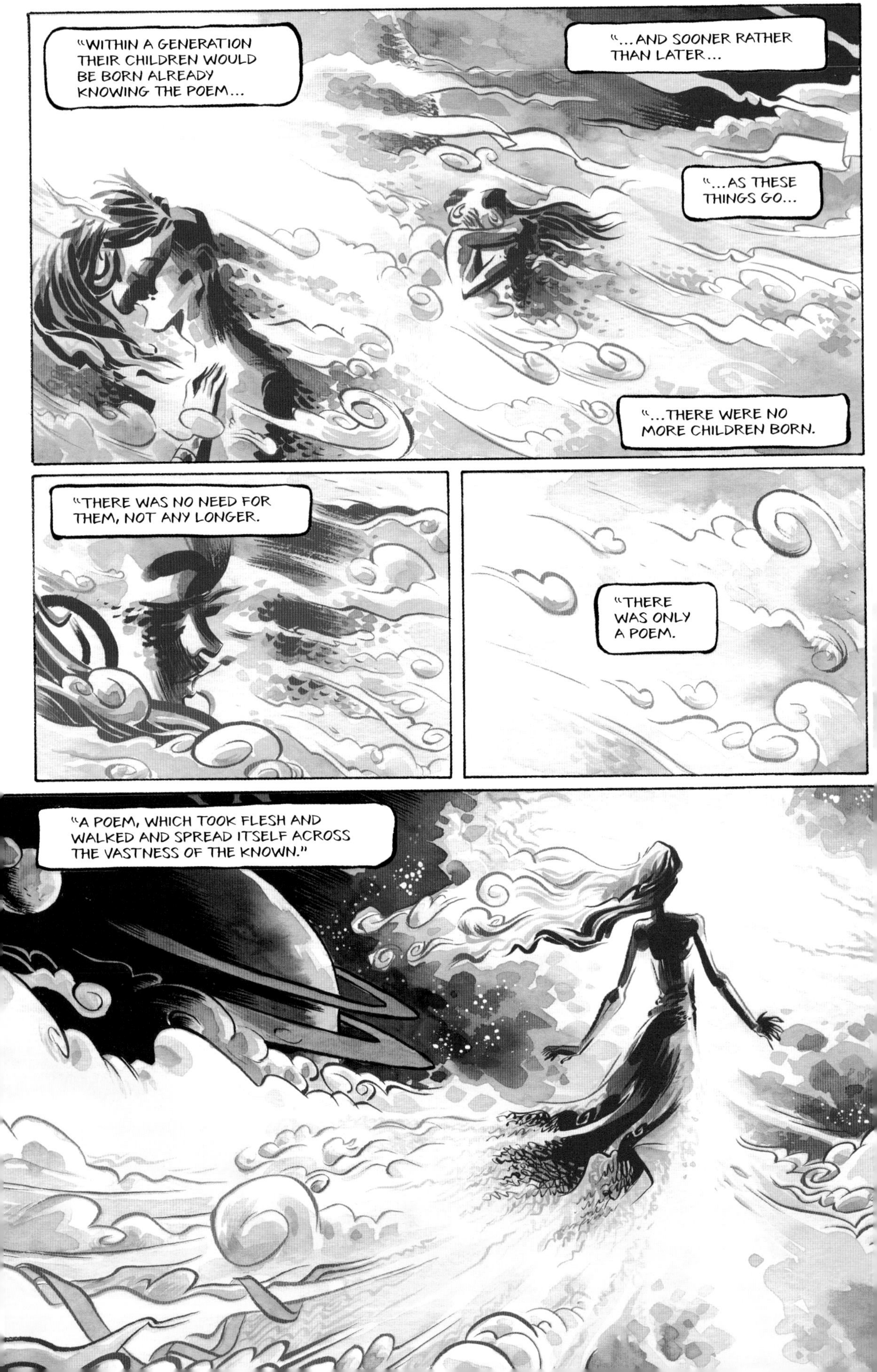
"WITHIN A GENERATION THEIR CHILDREN WOULD BE BORN ALREADY KNOWING THE POEM...
"...AND SOONER RATHER THAN LATER...
"...AS THESE THINGS GO...
"...THERE WERE NO MORE CHILDREN BORN.
"THERE WAS NO NEED FOR THEM, NOT ANY LONGER.
"THERE WAS ONLY A POEM.
"A POEM, WHICH TOOK FLESH AND WALKED AND SPREAD ITSELF ACROSS THE VASTNESS OF THE KNOWN."

THERE ARE PLACES...

...THAT WE ARE WELCOMED.

AND PLACES WHERE WE ARE REGARDED AS A NOXIOUS WEED...

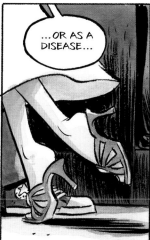

...OR AS A DISEASE...

...SOMETHING IMMEDIATELY TO BE QUARANTINED AND ELIMINATED.

BUT WHERE DOES CONTAGION END...

...AND ART BEGIN?

I DON'T...

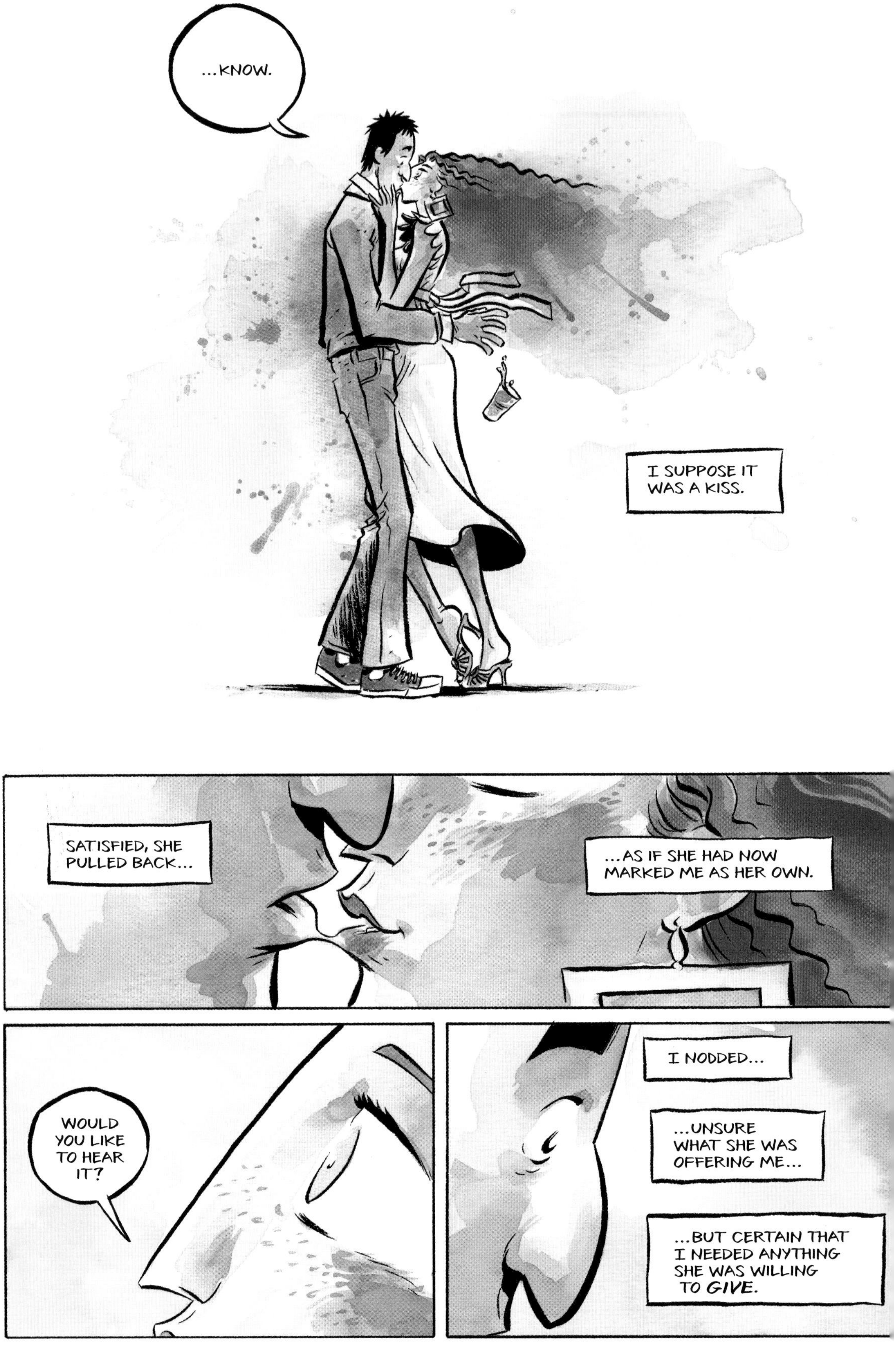

...KNOW.
I SUPPOSE IT WAS A KISS.
SATISFIED, SHE PULLED BACK...
...AS IF SHE HAD NOW MARKED ME AS HER OWN.
WOULD YOU LIKE TO HEAR IT?
I NODDED...
...UNSURE WHAT SHE WAS OFFERING ME...
...BUT CERTAIN THAT I NEEDED ANYTHING SHE WAS WILLING TO *GIVE*.

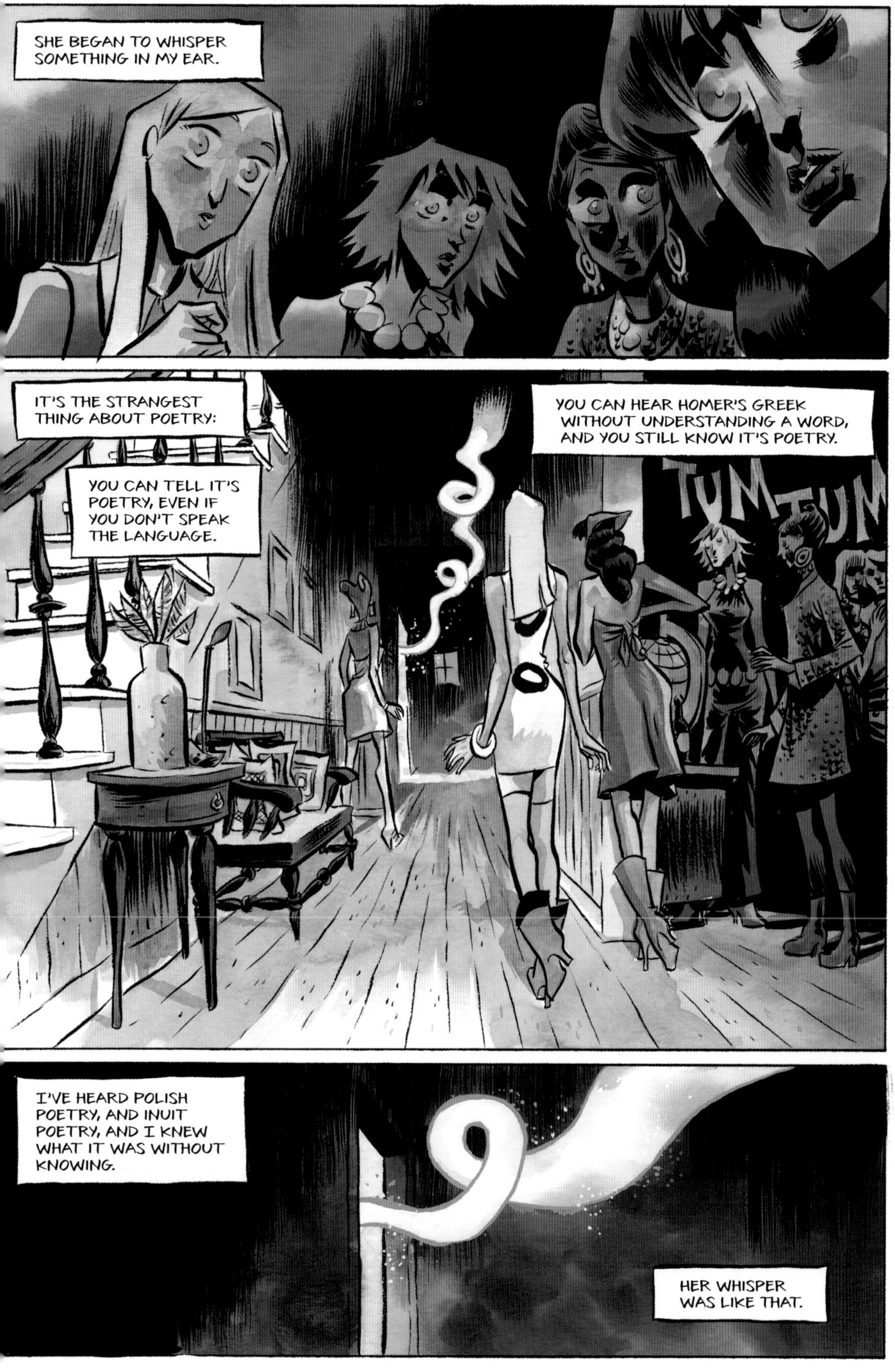
SHE BEGAN TO WHISPER SOMETHING IN MY EAR.
IT'S THE STRANGEST THING ABOUT POETRY:
YOU CAN TELL IT'S POETRY, EVEN IF YOU DON'T SPEAK THE LANGUAGE.
YOU CAN HEAR HOMER'S GREEK WITHOUT UNDERSTANDING A WORD, AND YOU STILL KNOW IT'S POETRY.
I'VE HEARD POLISH POETRY, AND INUIT POETRY, AND I KNEW WHAT IT WAS WITHOUT KNOWING.
HER WHISPER WAS LIKE THAT.

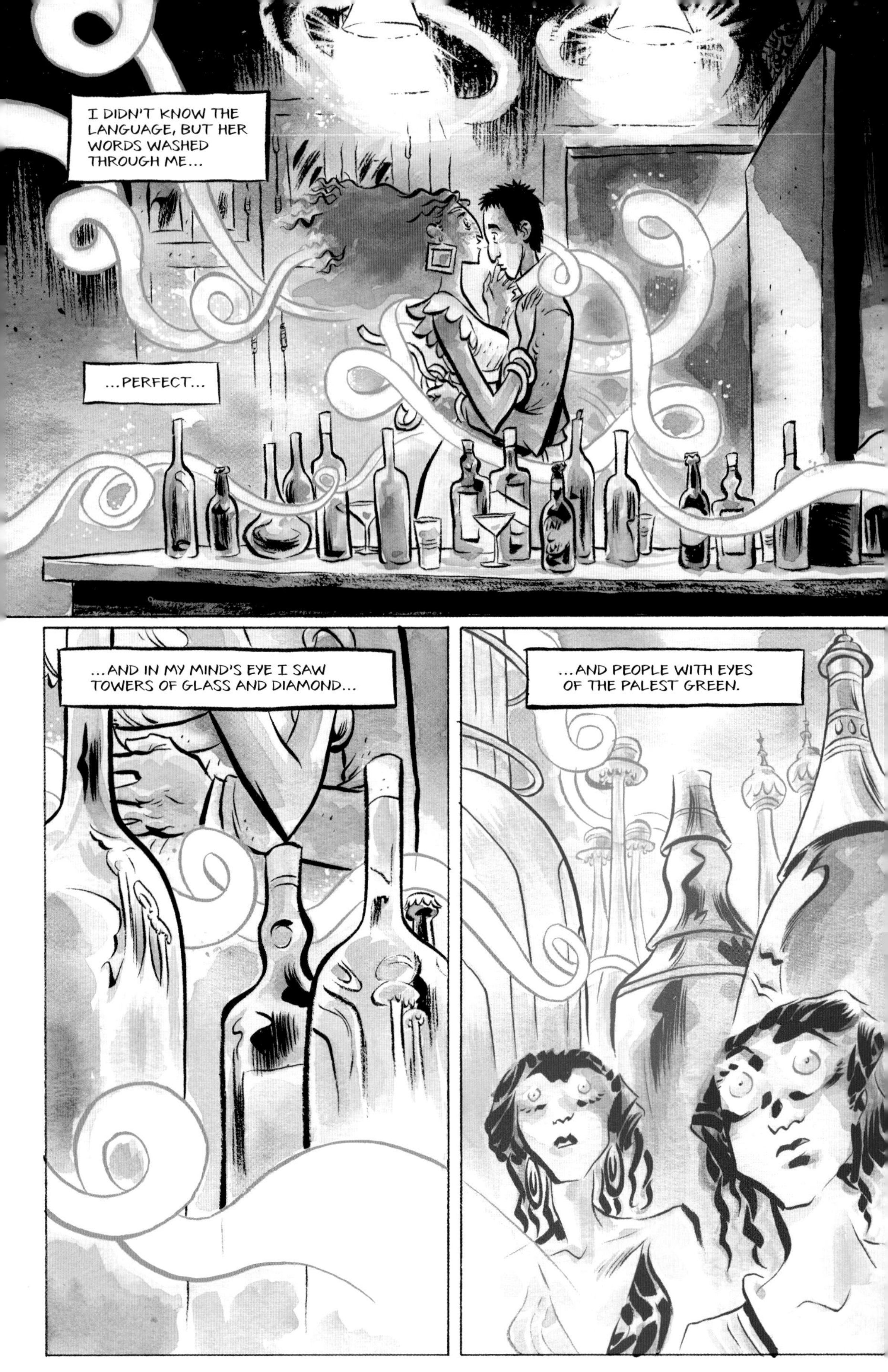
I DIDN'T KNOW THE LANGUAGE, BUT HER WORDS WASHED THROUGH ME...
...PERFECT...
...AND IN MY MIND'S EYE I SAW TOWERS OF GLASS AND DIAMOND...
...AND PEOPLE WITH EYES OF THE PALEST GREEN.

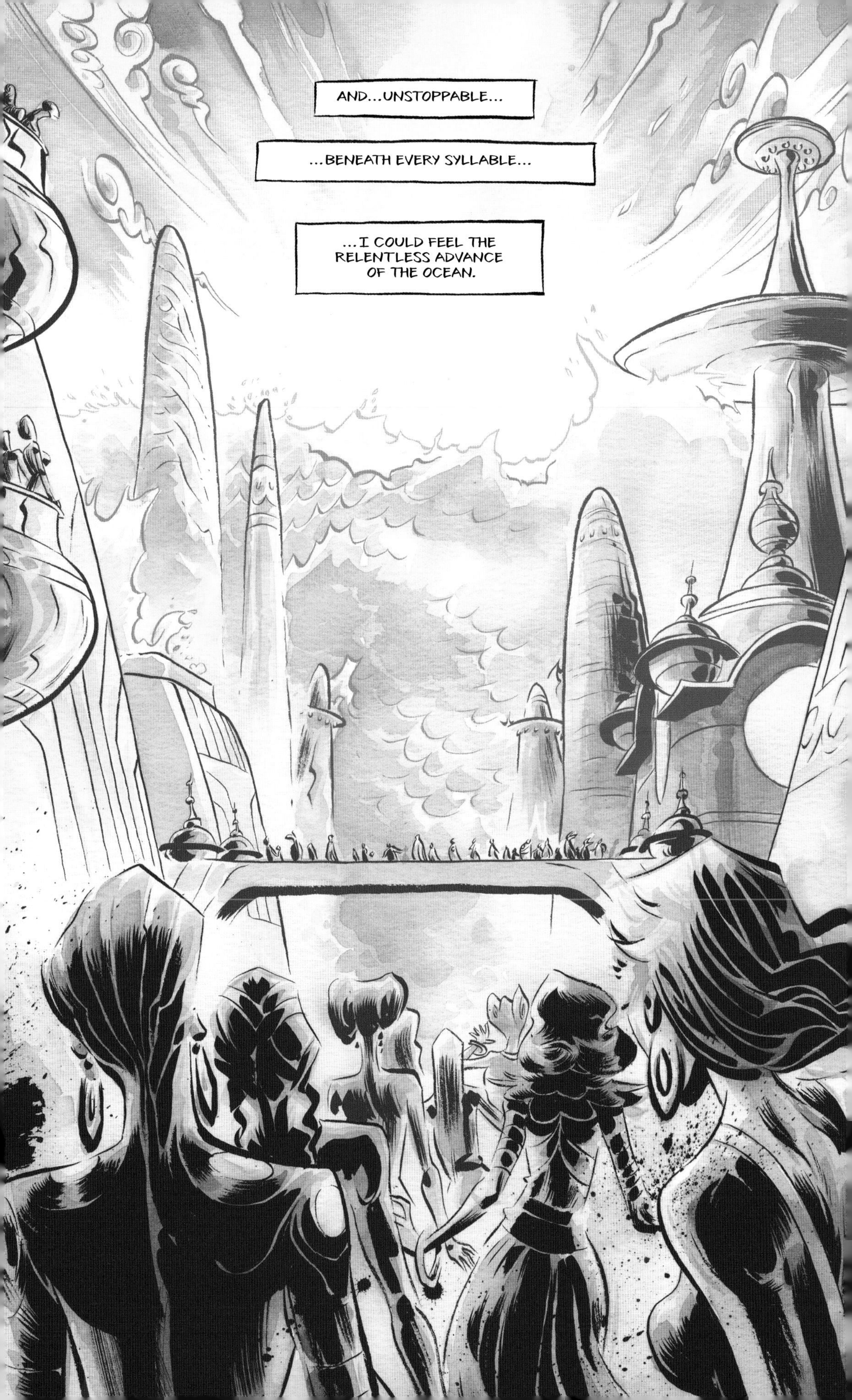
AND...UNSTOPPABLE...
...BENEATH EVERY SYLLABLE...
...I COULD FEEL THE RELENTLESS ADVANCE OF THE OCEAN.

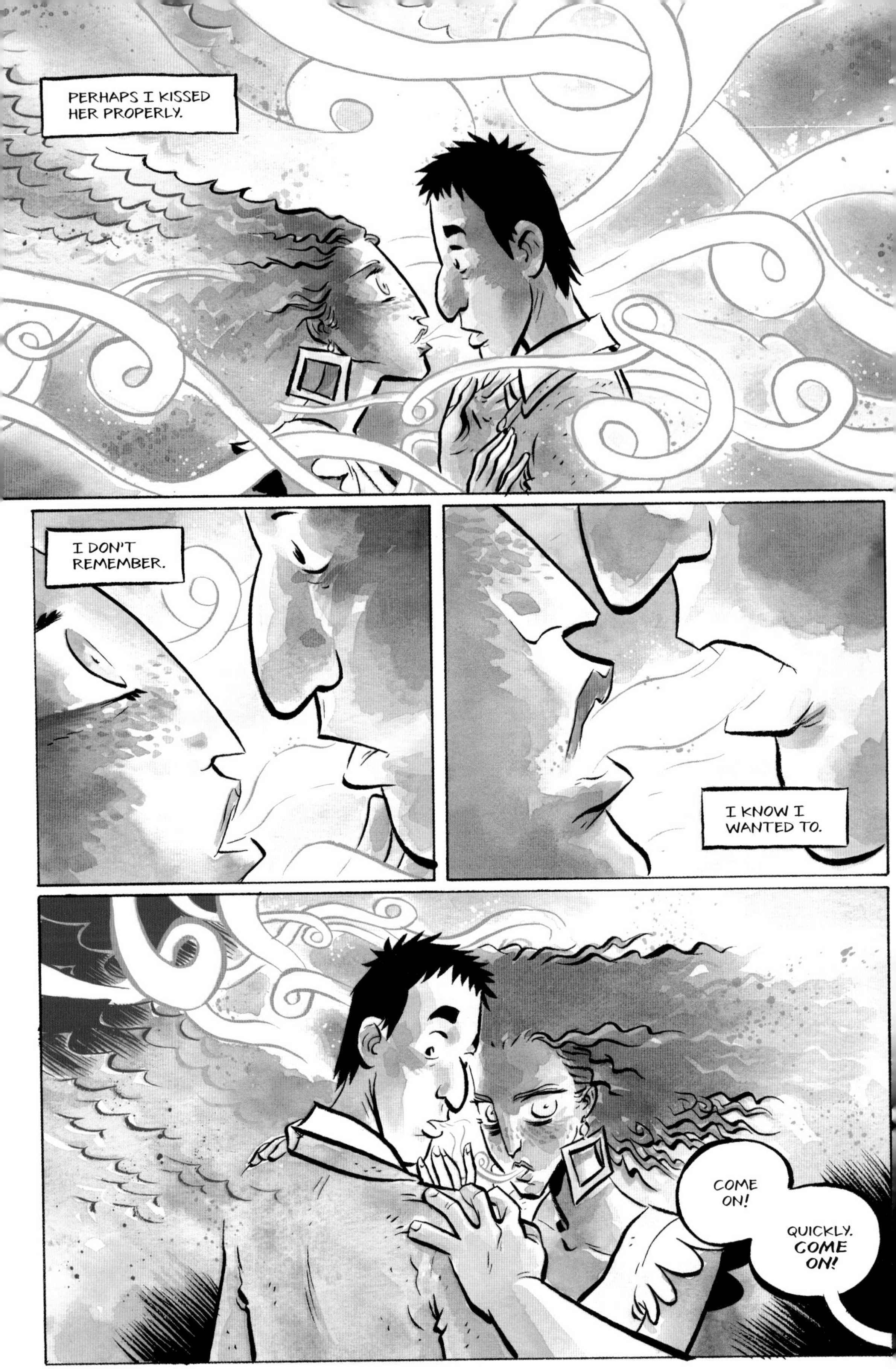
PERHAPS I KISSED HER PROPERLY.
I DON'T REMEMBER.
I KNOW I WANTED TO.
COME ON!
QUICKLY. COME ON!

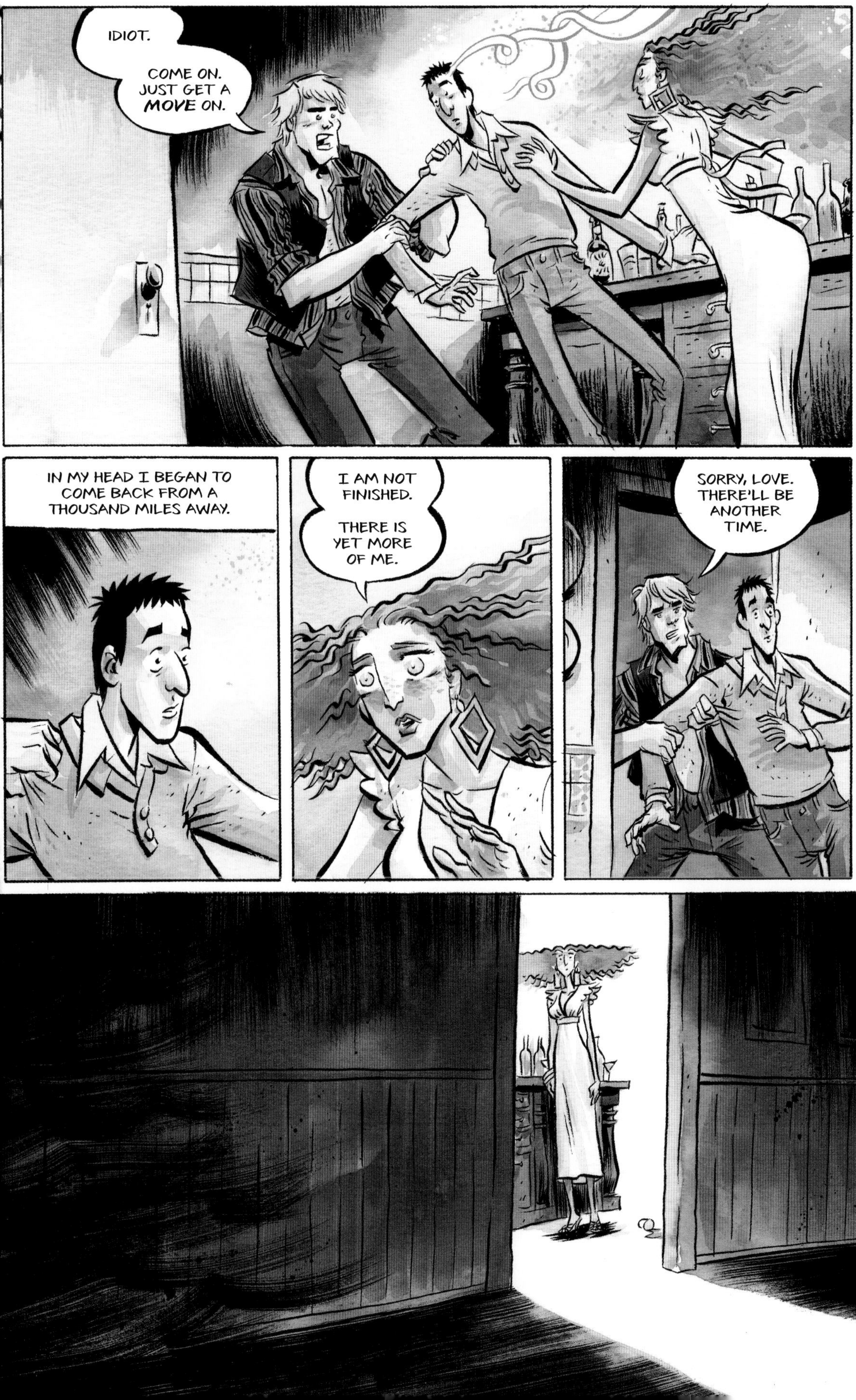
IDIOT.
COME ON. JUST GET A MOVE ON.
IN MY HEAD I BEGAN TO COME BACK FROM A THOUSAND MILES AWAY.
I AM NOT FINISHED.
THERE IS YET MORE OF ME.
SORRY, LOVE. THERE'LL BE ANOTHER TIME.

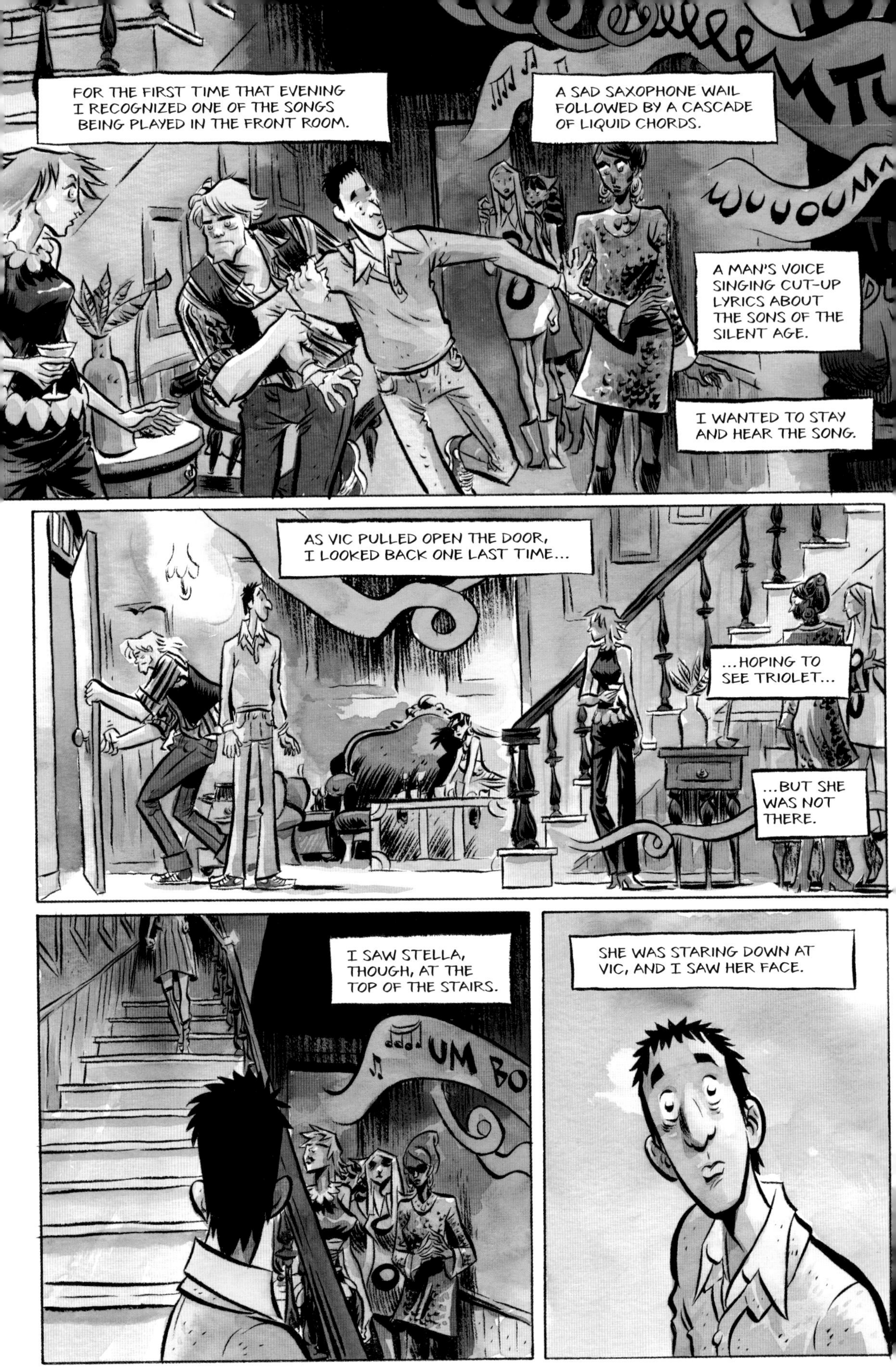
FOR THE FIRST TIME THAT EVENING I RECOGNIZED ONE OF THE SONGS BEING PLAYED IN THE FRONT ROOM.
A SAD SAXOPHONE WAIL FOLLOWED BY A CASCADE OF LIQUID CHORDS.
A MAN'S VOICE SINGING CUT-UP LYRICS ABOUT THE SONS OF THE SILENT AGE.
I WANTED TO STAY AND HEAR THE SONG.
AS VIC PULLED OPEN THE DOOR, I LOOKED BACK ONE LAST TIME...
...HOPING TO SEE TRIOLET...
...BUT SHE WAS NOT THERE.
I SAW STELLA, THOUGH, AT THE TOP OF THE STAIRS.
UM BO
SHE WAS STARING DOWN AT VIC, AND I SAW HER FACE.

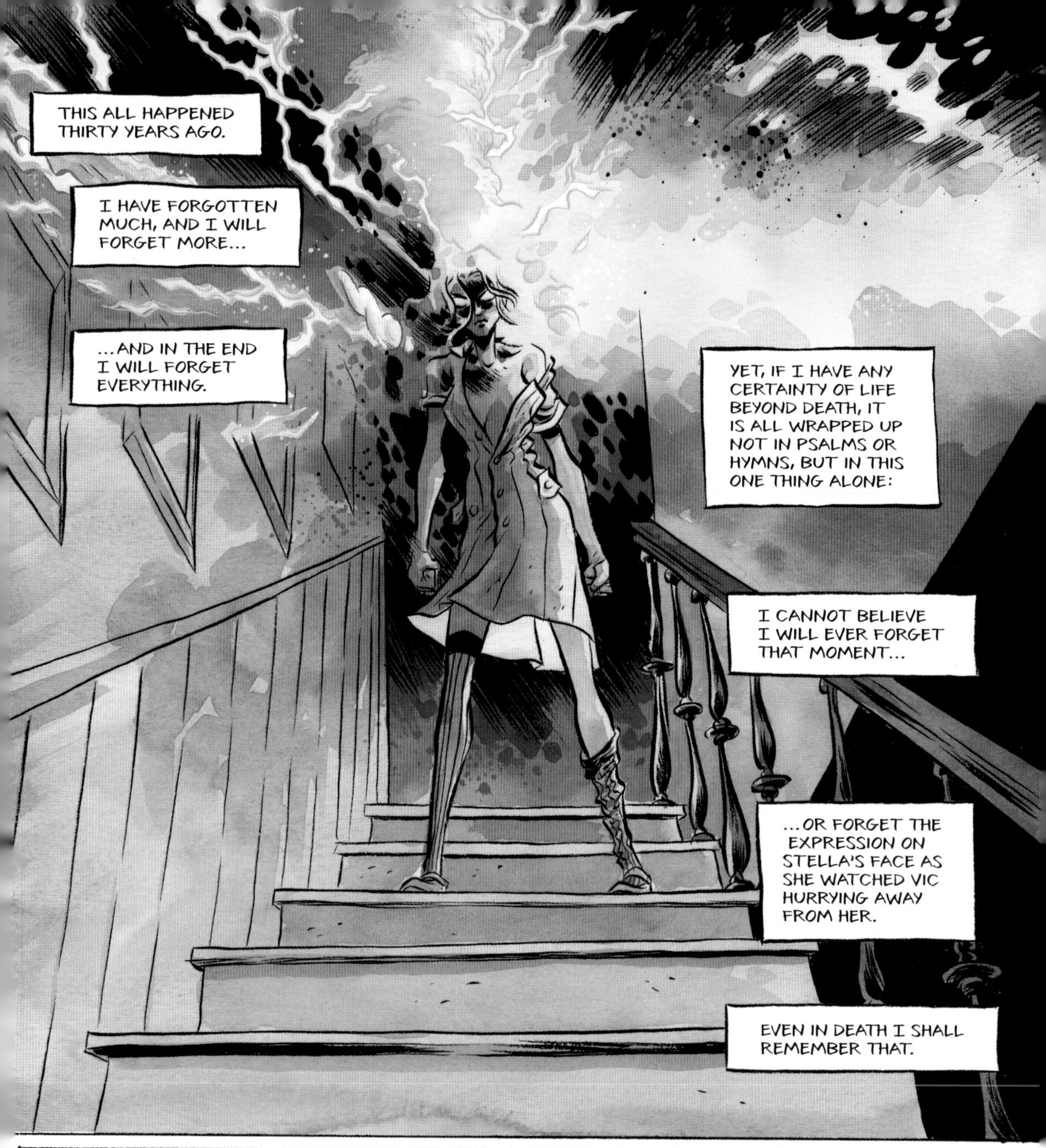
THIS ALL HAPPENED THIRTY YEARS AGO.
I HAVE FORGOTTEN MUCH, AND I WILL FORGET MORE...
...AND IN THE END I WILL FORGET EVERYTHING.
YET, IF I HAVE ANY CERTAINTY OF LIFE BEYOND DEATH, IT IS ALL WRAPPED UP NOT IN PSALMS OR HYMNS, BUT IN THIS ONE THING ALONE:
I CANNOT BELIEVE I WILL EVER FORGET THAT MOMENT...
...OR FORGET THE EXPRESSION ON STELLA'S FACE AS SHE WATCHED VIC HURRYING AWAY FROM HER.
EVEN IN DEATH I SHALL REMEMBER THAT.

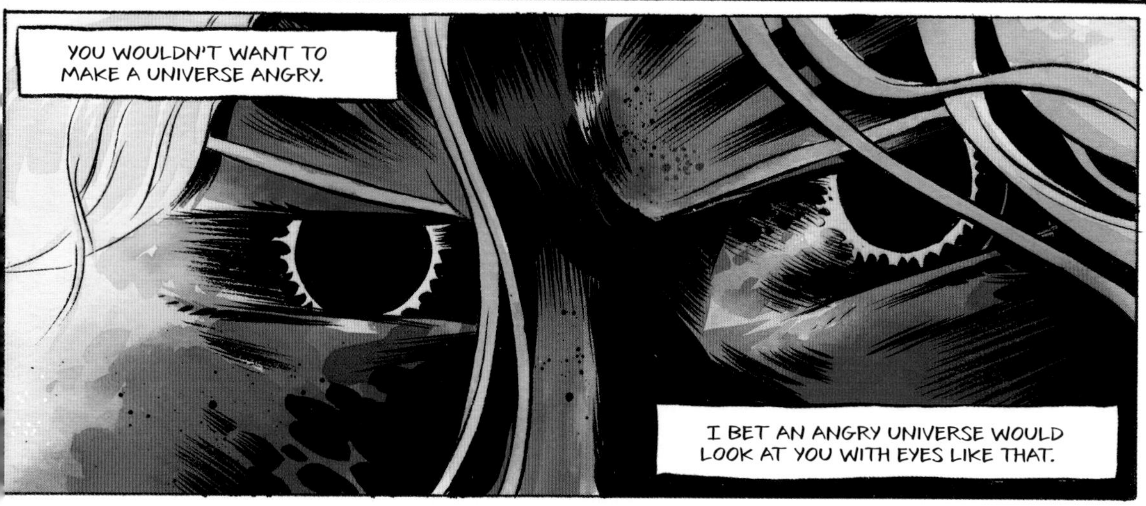
YOU WOULDN'T WANT TO MAKE A UNIVERSE ANGRY.
I BET AN ANGRY UNIVERSE WOULD LOOK AT YOU WITH EYES LIKE THAT.

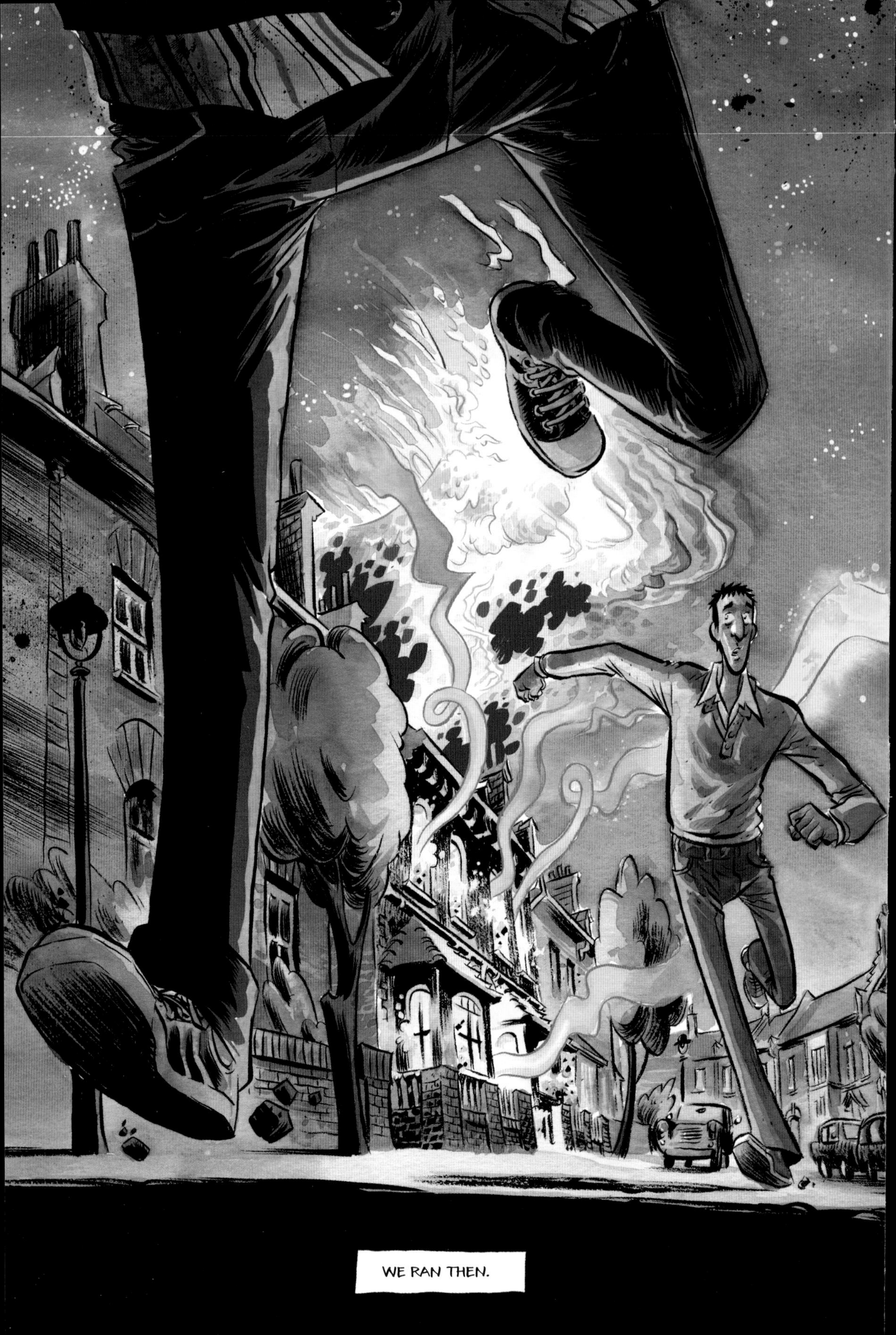
WE RAN THEN.

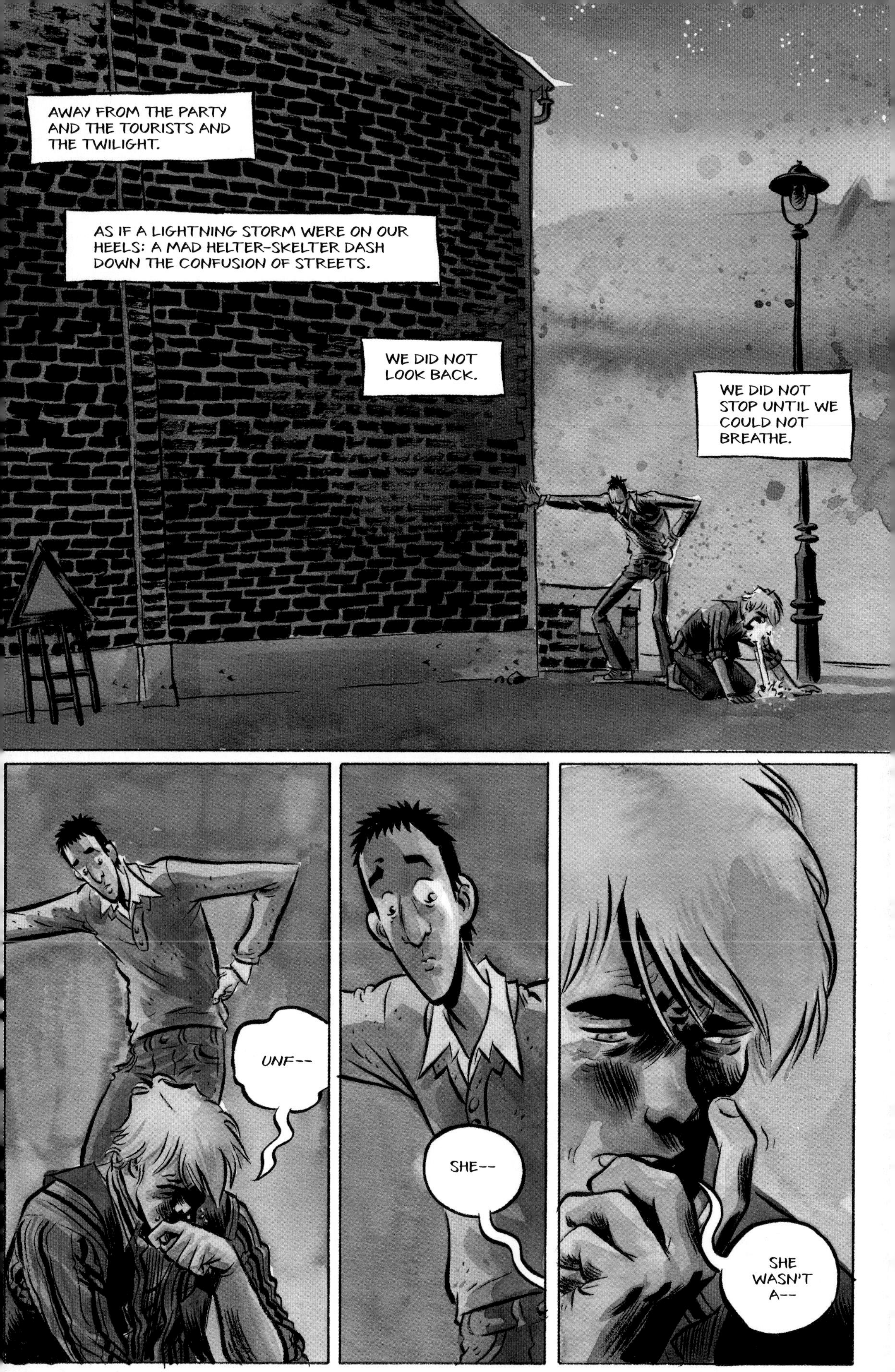
AWAY FROM THE PARTY AND THE TOURISTS AND THE TWILIGHT.
AS IF A LIGHTNING STORM WERE ON OUR HEELS: A MAD HELTER-SKELTER DASH DOWN THE CONFUSION OF STREETS.
WE DID NOT LOOK BACK.
WE DID NOT STOP UNTIL WE COULD NOT BREATHE.
UNF--
SHE--
SHE WASN'T A--

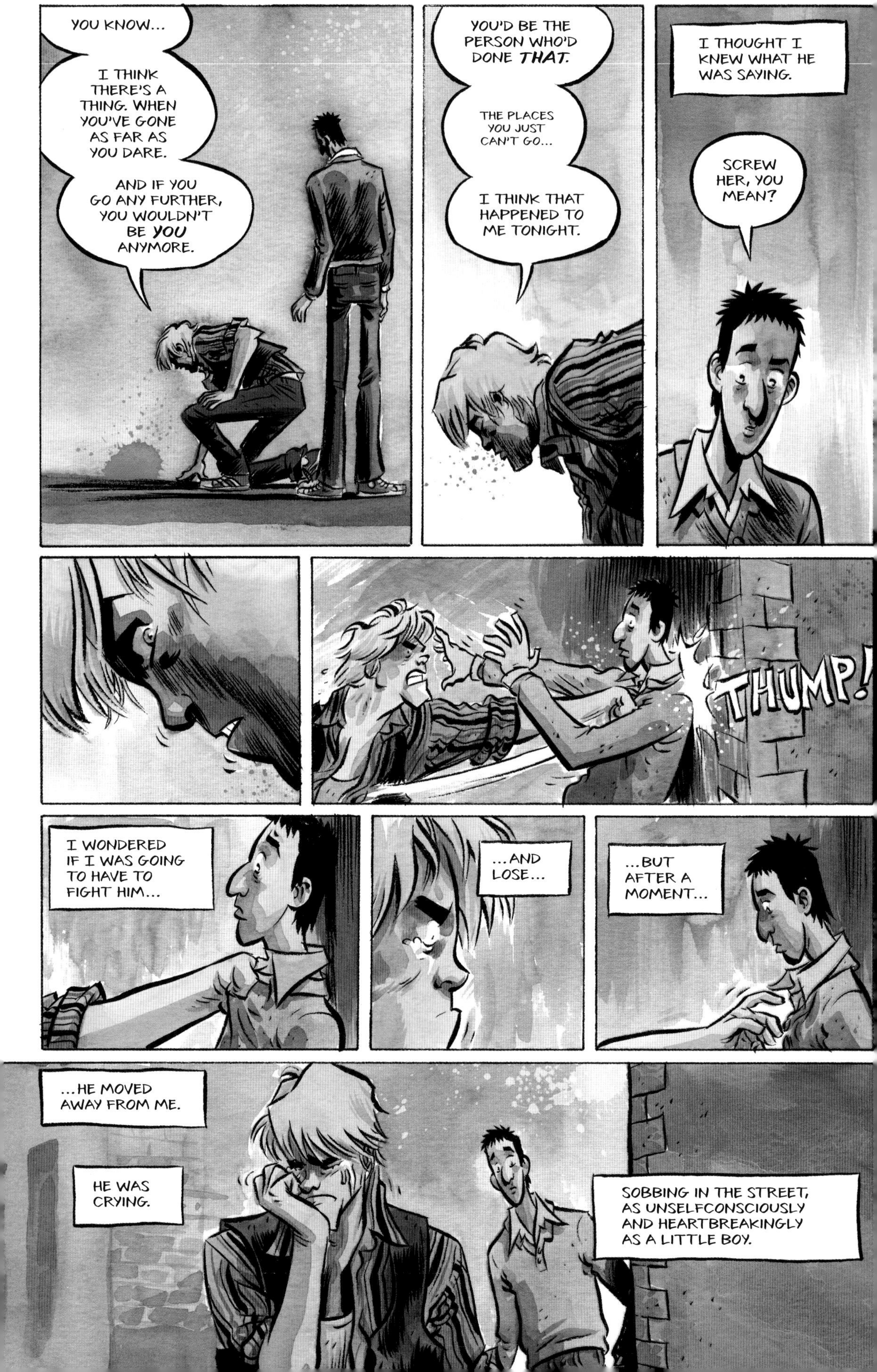
YOU KNOW...
I THINK THERE'S A THING. WHEN YOU'VE GONE AS FAR AS YOU DARE.
AND IF YOU GO ANY FURTHER, YOU WOULDN'T BE *YOU* ANYMORE.
YOU'D BE THE PERSON WHO'D DONE *THAT.*
THE PLACES YOU JUST CAN'T GO...
I THINK THAT HAPPENED TO ME TONIGHT.
I THOUGHT I KNEW WHAT HE WAS SAYING.
SCREW HER, YOU MEAN?
THUMP!
I WONDERED IF I WAS GOING TO HAVE TO FIGHT HIM...
...AND LOSE...
...BUT AFTER A MOMENT...
...HE MOVED AWAY FROM ME.
HE WAS CRYING.
SOBBING IN THE STREET, AS UNSELFCONSCIOUSLY AND HEARTBREAKINGLY AS A LITTLE BOY.

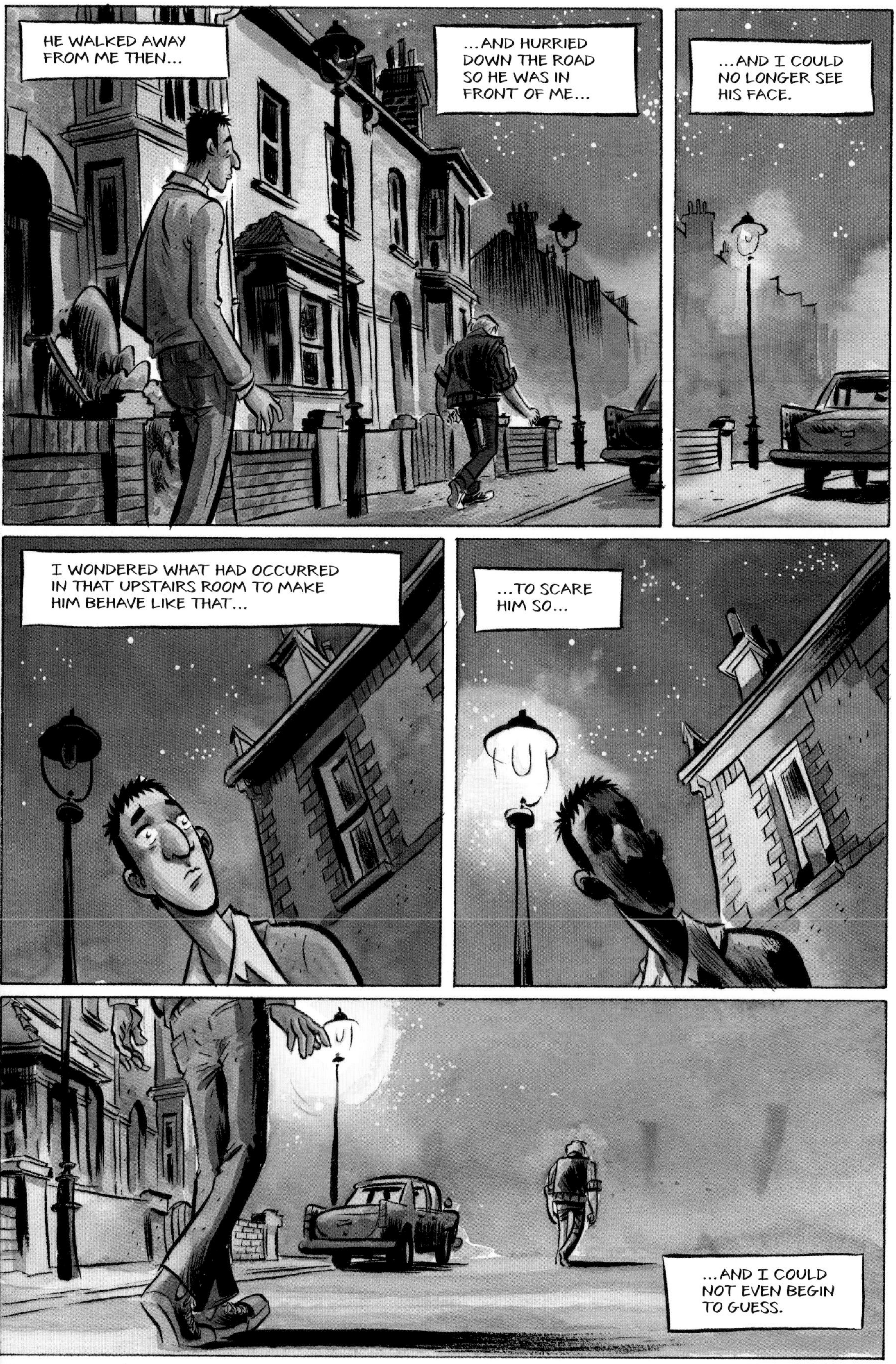
HE WALKED AWAY FROM ME THEN...
...AND HURRIED DOWN THE ROAD SO HE WAS IN FRONT OF ME...
...AND I COULD NO LONGER SEE HIS FACE.
I WONDERED WHAT HAD OCCURRED IN THAT UPSTAIRS ROOM TO MAKE HIM BEHAVE LIKE THAT...
...TO SCARE HIM SO...
...AND I COULD NOT EVEN BEGIN TO GUESS.

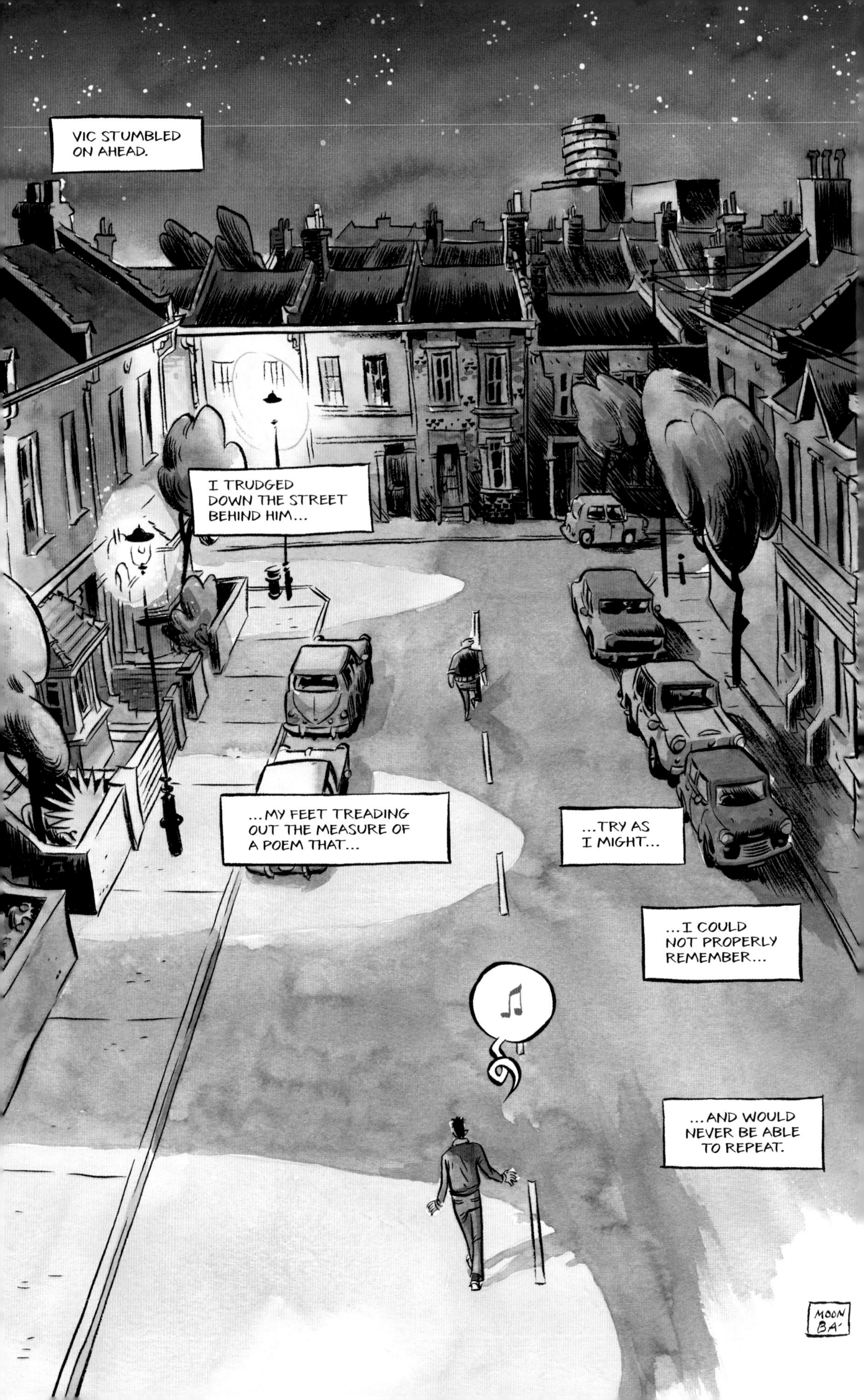
VIC STUMBLED ON AHEAD.
I TRUDGED DOWN THE STREET BEHIND HIM...
...MY FEET TREADING OUT THE MEASURE OF A POEM THAT...
...TRY AS I MIGHT...
...I COULD NOT PROPERLY REMEMBER...
...AND WOULD NEVER BE ABLE TO REPEAT.
MOON BÁ

Photo © Kimberly Butler

NEIL GAIMAN

Neil Gaiman is the author of over thirty acclaimed books and graphic novels for adults and children, including AMERICAN GODS, STARDUST, CORALINE, THE GRAVEYARD BOOK and TRIGGER WARNING: SHORT FICTIONS AND DISTURBANCES. His most recent novel for adults, THE OCEAN AT THE END OF THE LANE was highly acclaimed, appeared on the hardback and paperback *Sunday Times* bestseller lists and won several awards, including being voted Book of the Year in the National Book Awards 2013: 'Some books you read. Some books you enjoy. But some books just swallow you up, heart and soul' Joanne Harris.

The recipient of numerous literary honours, Neil Gaiman's work has been adapted for film, television and radio. He has written scripts for *Doctor Who*, collaborated with authors and illustrators including Terry Pratchett, Dave McKean and Chris Riddell, and THE SANDMAN (which garnered nine Eisner Awards and the World Fantasy Award for Best Short Story) is established as one of the classic graphic novels. As George R. R. Martin says: 'There's no one quite like Neil Gaiman.'

Originally from England, Neil Gaiman now lives in America.

🐦 @neilhimself

Photo by Keka Georgino

FÁBIO MOON & GABRIEL BÁ

Fábio Moon and Gabriel Bá are twin brothers born in 1976 in São Paulo, Brazil, where they live to this day. They have been telling stories in comic book form for over fifteen years, and their work has been published in twelve languages.

In 2007 they received their first Eisner Award nomination, for *De:Tales*, and the following year they won three Eisners for their work on *5*, *The Umbrella Academy*, and *Sugarshock!* Their 2010 limited series and magnum opus, *Daytripper*, garnered Eisner, Harvey, and Eagle awards, and went on to achieve great international acclaim through subsequent collections of the work.

The twins' most recent graphic novel, *Two Brothers*, has been touted as both 'another masterpiece' and 'a feat of bravura visual storytelling.' When not at the drawing board, the Brazilian wonder twins continue to travel around the world, sharing their great love for comics.